UNSENT

Penelope Shuttle has lived in Cornwall since 1970, is the widow of the poet Peter Redgrove, and has a grown-up daughter Zoe, who works in the field of sustainable energy.

Her first collection of poems, *The Orchard Upstairs* (1981) was followed by six other books from Oxford University Press, *The Child-Stealer* (1983), *The Lion from Rio* (1986), *Adventures with My Horse* (1988), *Taxing the Rain* (1994), *Building a City for Jamie* (1996) and *Selected Poems 1980-1996* (1998), and then *A Leaf Out of His Book* (1999) from Oxford Poets/Carcanet, and *Redgrove's Wife* (2006) and *Sandgrain and Hourglass* (2010) from Bloodaxe Books. *Redgrove's Wife* was shortlisted for both the Forward Prize and the T.S. Eliot Prize in 2006. *Sandgrain and Hourglass* is a Poetry Book Society Recommendation. Her latest book, *Unsent: New & Selected Poems 1980-2012* (Bloodaxe Books, 2012), is drawn from ten collections published over three decades plus a new collection, *Unsent*.

First published as a novelist, her fiction includes *All the Usual Hours of Sleeping* (1969), *Wailing Monkey Embracing a Tree* (1973) and *Rainsplitter in the Zodiac Garden* (1977).

With Peter Redgrove, she is co-author of *The Wise Wound: Menstruation and Everywoman* (1978) and *Alchemy for Women: Personal Transformation Through Dreams and the Female Cycle* (1995), as well as a collection of poems, *The Hermaphrodite Album* (1973), and two novels, *The Terrors of Dr Treviles: A Romance* (1974) and *The Glass Cottage: A Nautical Romance* (1976).

Shuttle's work is widely anthologised and can be heard on The Poetry Archive Website. Her poetry has been broadcast on BBC Radio 3 and 4, and her poem 'Outgrown' was used recently in a radio and television commercial. She has been a judge for many poetry competitions, is a Hawthornden Fellow, and a tutor for the Poetry School. She is current Chair of the Falmouth Poetry Group, one of the longest-running poetry workshops in the country.

PENELOPE SHUTTLE

UNSENT

NEW & SELECTED POEMS 1980-2012

BLOODAXE BOOKS

ISBN: 978 1 85224 950 2

First published 2012 by
Bloodaxe Books Ltd,
Highgreen,
Tarset,
Northumberland NE48 1RP.

www.bloodaxebooks.com
For further information about Bloodaxe titles
please visit our website or write to
the above address for a catalogue.

Supported using public funding by
**ARTS COUNCIL
ENGLAND**

Cover design: Neil Astley & Pamela Robertson-Pearce.

Printed in Great Britain by
Bell & Bain Limited, Glasgow, Scotland.

For my mother Joan and for my daughter Zoe
and in memory of Peter Redgrove and Jack Shuttle

ACKNOWLEDGEMENTS

This edition includes poems selected from these books by Penelope Shuttle: *The Orchard Upstairs* (1980), *The Child-Stealer* (1983), *The Lion from Rio* (1986), *Adventures with My Horse* (1988), *Taxing the Rain* (1992) and *Building a City for Jamie* (1996), all published by Oxford University Press; *A Leaf Out of His Book* (Oxford Carcanet, 1999); *Redgrove's Wife* (2006) and *Sandgrain and Hourglass* (2010), both published by Bloodaxe Books.

Acknowledgements are due to the editors of the following publications in which some of the new poems in the *Unsent* (2012) section of the book first appeared: *Agenda, Artemis, The Manhattan Review, Necessary Steps, Poetry Review, The Rialto, Temenos* and *The Yellow Nib*. I am indebted to Roddy Lumsden's poem 'Quietus' for the phrase 'third wish of three'.

CONTENTS

from ADVENTURES WITH MY HORSE (1988)

from TAXING THE RAIN (1992)

The Orchard Upstairs

(1980)

Eavesdropper

Here is your face
wintering in a photograph,
alive and alone

I look at it,
at you as you were then,
and the midsummer opens,

pale feathers of ice fall
from the sky around me
and nearby, the ocean,

like a ghost's throat,
grows translucent.

Skeletals

Three skeletals are climbing
out of their blue and gold boxes.
They lift the lids of their coffins
and clamber out, naked,
each ribcage a cuirass of bone.
The central corpse
lifts up his arms in astonished blessing.
Behind him,
a tapestry of three-petalled flowers
flourishes,
trinity behind trinity.

And the celebration goes on,
the joyful pillage of golden light,
the rescue from a long deep dark,
the arrival into unfading colour
from the fastness of the sepulchre.

Three Lunulae, Truro Museum

Gold so thin,
only an old woman
would notice its weight

Crescent moons of gold
from the sunken district
of the dark,
out of the archaeologist's earth

The women of the lunulae
threw no barbaric shadows
yet a vivid dance
lit up their bones

I sense the mood
of many women
who wore the new moon
like a necklace

They have got over
the winter
while I still freeze

The slight quick tap
of a clock
goes on

like the rhythm
of an insect's leg
in the grass

I linger
in the locked room
of the gold,

trying to see,
beyond the sickle shapes,
the faces of three women

Sharp shadows breathe hard,
shedding skins like dusty snakes
Light twists in a violent retching

For an instant
there is the fragment of a lip,
an eyebrow fine as a spider's threat

A face like a frost fern

The custodian
locks the lunulae
in the safe once more

Cornish, they are,
he says,
dug up at St Juliot,
regalia of this soil,
and not for the British Museum

You buy me
a postcard of the lunulae
and we leave the museum,
enter the thin gold remains
of autumn

Rain

There is the thunder again
The rain falls
on the houses full of bags of bones
No one cuts flowers
The empty promises of the month
flush down beneath the streets,
through drains
The dots and dashes of the rain
are a waterlogged code

I am in the conscript army of summer
The rain dowses my fingerprints
Roses shudder, even the limbs of trees ache

On the shelf, the books are stern as cloud
I cannot read them

The rain stands miles apart from all the bibles
overcoming words with its own saturating argot

Appletree in America

An appletree by the roadside
and the road five hours travelling
out of New York City.

Here's a frontier,
this tree ripening
and the windfalls on the ground
like a first furnishing
in a continent
where I flit like a ghost
unanchored at twilight.

I hold a branch
and smell the apples,
watersweet, a beginning,
opening of energies
to rouse me from homesickness
as, beyond the roadside tree,
these foreign fields and hills
merge into the familiar loam of evening.

Honesty

What are these papery flowers,
thin stiff petals dry as insects,
these plants that rustle

as I pick them? Dry dilemmas,
arranged in a glass of water,
they go on puzzling me.

For days they are quite still,
unchanging.
They will not move in any breeze.

I see these nameless oval wafers
as if in an offing,
the most distant part of the sea
visible from the shore.

But when I touch their dry membranes,
they do not resist,
only fade and disintegrate,
finding the end of their pallor.

They are not unapproachable.
My mother says they are called 'honesty'.

Glass-maker

It is no skill of mine,
glass-making.
I apprehend none of its craft,
transparency wiser than gardens.

To make glass
is clearer communication than speech.
A woman-maker of windows,
how would she look?

Angrily, piercingly at you
through her own upstairs window?
Or would she be smooth, hairless,
all bone, glabella?

Arduous manufacture, glass,
yet so simple to break.
Just strike it a glancing blow
and see the fragments, petal-less.

Are there glass-makers
on Arcturus or Aldebaran?
Does sun there sheer off unknown windows,
create blinding mirrors?

Dress me in glass!
Shoes, sleeves, all...
Let me move with great care,
interned in glass garments,
until I become glass.
my body made of glass,
cool and irreversible change,
glass eyebrow,
fingernail, clitoris...

Bone, blood and breath: all glass.
Until I am a devotee of glass,
reflecting all its famishings.

Downpour

A strong rain falls, a bony downpour.
The waters roar, like a riddance.
The day vanishes suddenly
and it is night that hesitates on a brink
for fear of difficulties. The rain, for instance.

Through the letter box, leaves instead of letters,
wet leaves blown along the path
and seeping through the low letter box,
an invasion that comes slowly,
but helped by the rain. The downpour.

I dream of thorns, aeroplanes and red horses,
but seldom of rain.
The creature spinning webs to catch its prey,
I dream of her also
but almost never of rain. The webs of rain.

The rain does not slacken. It has the scent
of mistletoe. But it is a weapon, thrown.
The windows shine black with it.
I sit watching the knotted bunches of rain.
I do not want to cease watching. Such brawny rain.

But the dry house, its music and its meals,
recalls me from the window,
draws me back from a downpour that is drowning me.
I prepare to turn from the window,
yet remain a moment longer,
looking at the blur of the candle-flame
against the dark glass.

There is the downpour. Here is the uprush of light.

November Poppies

I post my letters
and turn from the town,
from the wild children
in the schoolyard,
to the sea
and the first darkness
coming down on the water,
down from the harbour hill
unstoppable
like a young rider
clinging to the back
of his terrified horse.
The hills across the bay
are the colour of slate roofs,
blue and grey,
and watching them I hear
the winter earth echoing,
I hear it reading its sun and moon letters.
Again the twilight wind
menaces the water.
I open my mouth to taste its coldness
that leaves no poison on my tongue.

An hour later, I open my door.
I hope for a friend to join me,
to talk and joke.
But it is a stranger on the threshold,
an old woman with envious eyes
lifting towards me her reproachful tray,
offering me hundreds of poppies,
the reek of remembrance.

Four American Sketches

The Blind

The sun outstares me.
I pull down the blind.
Under these old afternoon clothes
my scarf-skin quivers.
My skin is thin and dry
like certain plants
and I fear the approach of my stronger self,
that reflection
who will flay me
until the flaps of my skin
bang like blinds
in a wind that doesn't care.

One of the Narrations

These shrubs are unmarred by autumn.
A thousand narrations
might spring from their neighbourliness,
by my window.

But the shadow of my opponent
who wears my own inaccurate face
reaches out from unexpected hiding places,
ending my repose,
dragging me to sad locations
on the other side of the candle.

Here the autumn hobbles me.
All is cloudiness and the antagonist's hug.
We are face to face, she and I.
My dark side is towards the earth.

That New Moon

That new moon waiting for me
to step out into twilight
is no desolate island:

Not that little moon
around which the minnowy-blue sky flows,
no.

Nor is that new moon
made of snow.

That moon has the strength of a million spines.
It is this moon alone which stays awake all night.

November First, New York State

Spurges, cascarilla, cassava:
the steepings of November,
mild disrobings, a damp natural air,
a day of reprieve.
A sour cold waits its turn
but today the mazes of autumn revolve.
Our personal effects are wedged into bright rooms,
the windows are wide open,
breathing the almost extinct summer.
You and I are reading the bibliotheca of autumn.

Cupboard Hyacinths

In the cupboard under the stairs
the winter flowers are crooning
in their cardboard pots.

In the fierce dark
the roots of the hyacinth are stretching
their green havoc.

I sit on the stairs
thinking of the garden beneath me
in the underworld of the cupboard.

I think how handsome
my hyacinths will be,
how they will tower over December
with a fragrance as heavy as Isis.

I will keep their corms from pestilence
because they contain my answers,
Without the bending Pisas of their stems
I will have too many questions.

I wait by the cupboard door,
I want to hear them grow,
I want to experience the cupboard's weather.

I want to carry my blossoming lamps
into the winter rooms,
their odour a guttural equilibrium
settling everything once and for all.

'The World has Passed'

On the other side of the rose
there is the felling of trees

On the other side of the frost
there is the colour of a bruise

On the other side of the ovum
there is the woman of warfare

On the other side of the bonfire
there is the music springing back,
the retaliation

On the other side of the leaf
is the lesson in lacemaking

On the other side of the room
is a cabinet of curiosities, antique granary

On the other side of the mother
is a sigh full of filaments,
a few words walking on tiptoe

On the other side of the blackberry
is the harvest of the moon

On the other side of the voice
is the absence of the waterfall

On the other side of the ice
is the half-satisfied sea

On the other side of the blood
is the unrooted child

On the other side of the child
is the gulping-down of cloud,
the whispering of loopholes –
arrival at last at the fresh shrine

TITLE: *Yokut*, Native American term for 'a year has gone by'.

25

The Conceiving

(for Zoe)

Now
you are in the ark of my blood
in the river of my bones
in the woodland of my muscles
in the ligaments of my hair
in the wit of my hands
in the smear of my shadow
in the armada of my brain
under the stars of my skull
in the arms of my womb
Now you are here
you worker in the gold of flesh

Expectant Mother

In the stillness,
uterine,
hidden from me,
hidden from mirrors,
the foetal roots of wrist
and heart
are coiled within me.
They belong to the child,
to the incast,
a plumage of constellations.

I walk around the house
in bare feet
and a warm rope of blood
links me to my child

Rain falls on gardens and inscriptions
but I hold the edge of the rain.
I am a receptacle
in which other rain, amniotic, gathers,
for the one in his official residence
to enjoy.

I think of the quiet use of the unborn eyelids
and the stillness of my breasts that swell up,
a warm procedure of strength.

Already a name suggests its syllables,
but this remains secret,
a fishtail shadow,
a whisper between the night and the day.

First Foetal Movements of My Daughter, Summer 1976

Shadow of a fish
The water-echo
Inner florist dancing
Her fathomless ease
Her gauzy thumbs
Leapfrogger,
her Olympics in the womb's stadium

The Orchard Upstairs

1

Here I meet no king-killer
Here I throw no shadow
Before birth, before the present tense,
I moved here amid darks, lunar dusk,
a ferret of blood, the unborn,
fenestella

2

Outside, the wind and the rain,
a darkness lurching against the threadbare house:
inside, the orchard upstairs

But I do not understand these fruits yet

3

Around the moon,
my dreams cluster, not moths
The antique photographs of the dreams
lead me always to this one room,
overlooking neglected lawn and pond

From a window I look down again
at the leafy air-raid shelter,
hear again steam trains shunting beyond the trees

Opening a door to a room in which apples are stored
in rows, I hear the stark cries of a woman giving birth

4

The room was cold, as if no glass
were fixed in the window frames
The room was damp, as if a fountain
sprang in the centre of the room
The room was draughty,
as if the house was fallen in ruins

I stand at the threshold,
lunar observer at the brink of apples

5

In the unused room
she laid out the windfall apples in rows
The silent house was filled with the scent of bruised apples
I climb the stairs
of a familiar house whose demolition approaches
My bones break with the bricks,
the foundations of my heart will crack

6

Something, a cloth, a veil?
chokes me
The doorways throb, like yew branches
in a storm
The old house eavesdrops
It bewails my thoughts

7

I do not sleep in this bedroom any more
But I shed skins here
I touch the skin of an apple
It is smooth as the ear of a hare

8

A woman in childbirth,
the difficult fame of labour
All night, all day, all night again:
the freshly-painted walls of the nursery
echo with her whorling cries

At dawn, a newborn howling amid
the apples of the future

9

The leaves scud before the wind
across the lawn,
leaves like birthmarks

10

A small speck or stain
on my heart,

it is my sadness for the lost room,
the pillaged house

What are the conditions for equilibrium?
Is there a balance among apples?

    11

Like bone the stairs that I climb
and ice the banisters I grasp
Is it a garden of fruit trees I approach,
or is it a cemetery
    And the brightness of colour,
       is it life or death,
          that red?

    12

In the morning, the sun cools itself
against the orchard mirror
I sit on the window ledge
and below me the lawn is calm green water,
a lake of old love

The Child-Stealer

(1983)

Twilight

The twilight
is like a fine rain
forcing us home.

Under the trees
glow the chalky threads
of snowdrops

at which I stare –
who goes there,
the sentry cries.

But how can I describe
the mastery of flowers
grazing the earth,

like translations done
without dictionaries?

Wings

On me
are beating the invisible wings
of the firstborn,
unique
as a distillate
of all the languages

and they are also
the heavy wings of stone
that pull me down
from my happy sojourn in the air
and drag me to the ground

I gasp and the hoop of breath
bowls me along

The Buds

In the ancient fuchsia bushes
there are always bees,
at any time of day.
The bushes are so old
they are turning into trees,
the stem of each bush
hardening into a gnarled trunk.
The pendulous scarlet-mauve blossoms
call the bees with their scents,
tuning-forks to the bee-songs.
My young daughter and her friend
pop the new buds in their firm fingers.
In response to my rebuke
they tell me, seriously,
that this helps the buds to grow.

Indoors and Outdoors

Listen, the snow-sheaves are rustling,
a frozen harvest.

And quietly, the snow is speaking.
Snow refuses to stand trial.

No matter,
indoors the furnaces are ready.

They roar in the basements,
enraged ancestors.

I listen to the sly ifs of fire.
I dance on hot coals,
skid over thin ice.

Indoors, the snow is afraid of me.
Outdoors, I fear the calamity of cold,
unignitable enemy.

Grosser ice encases the few twigs
of the thin bush by the back door.
The bird's abandoned nest
is thonged with ice.

Winter inherits the outdoors.
Indoors the fires are making themselves at home.

Märchen
or, The Earthborn

Our smart house new-painted chocolate brown
makes me think too closely of the Märchen,
of Hansel and Gretel, and the tasty roof;
of the maiden with no hands;
and all the dangerous defenceless ones
in those old and far-off tales.

Birds that were girls and boys,
bears and foxes that once were men;
girls who crouch in the kitchen ashes,
golden gowns hidden in nutshells,
these cruel and vengeful heroes and heroines.
In this half-light of a winter afternoon
I pity the old parents warily watching
their gleaming half-human young.

In an Old Garden
Lanhydrock House, Cornwall

A pewter urn
crammed with blue flowers
presided over
by two infant angels
brooding, chins sunk in cupped hands,

elbows propped
on the urn's discoloured rim.
Day after day they gaze
at these flowers,
sun baking their pewter wings,
rain dripping down
their cherub backs.
Buttocks perched
on sprays of iron leaves,
they freeze in winter,
but never lift their heads
from precarious contemplation.

No one disturbs their repose,
their steadfast response to the flowers
The motionless sweetness of the twai
rules the garden like an enchantment

Not born yet, my child,
my little dancer, equilibrist,
ever-mobile creature,
who will laugh at their solemn pose; dance,
and leave their spell unbroken,
the garden sustained by her guiltless glance.

Nude Study

Deep in it her skin
has that faint light left
when the sun has just gone
below the horizon.
She does not expect
not to be scrutinised.
For some she walks through the forest
following the tracks of the beloved,
touching wood all the time.
For others she is an echo of poverty.
Or she is simply statuesque, motionless
on her plinth,
maybe a dweller in heaven, maybe not.

She offers herself to some
like a scroll of ancient design;
to others as an old tax-demand envelope
covered with doodles.
For release she has only to speak.
This action will bring her freedom,
meagre, plain, bare liberty.
It is not indecorous to ask for this.
But neither is it dangerous to have her body displayed,
her silence unbroken,
her bones kept still for our enquiries,
the breasts casual, the knees braced.
Today her smile is uninflected,
neither listless nor deliberately appealing;
with arms upraised and pelvis tilted contemplatively,
she is utterly visible, perfectly eloquent.

Disembarkation

This white ship sails on a crimson sea.
There are no storms.

I crawl along the deck, peer in terror
over the polished taffrail.
This is no pleasure cruise.

There are no deckchairs in red and white striped canvas.
No traveller sips bouillon.
There is certainly no anchor.

A scarlet wake flares out behind us
and the ocean of red glows like grease.
My skin is like a statue of me.
Even if an ogre, the captain is invisible.

His ship's prow guts the ocean
as if each wave were a fish.
His ship crosses the seas, flat red lawns.
Always, this journey across leafless red,
the ship leap-frogging on.

Yet now it slows, sighs deep in its engines,
even this ship sighs, retchingly, and slows.
Stars, nebulae, appear in the sky.
And here are the lights of the land.

The ship loses its vigour
and all that strength comes to me!

Knowing nothing but strength, I jump for it.
Beneath my feet, the waves of clay dip,
almost throwing me to the ground.
I struggle to get my balance, gasp for air,
inhale the different bacillae of dry land.

(Out on the horizon, that ship,
the frigate of blood,
sails on over the humble water,
forever bound on its sluggish voyage.)

Preference

Preferring flowers,
I acknowledge meridians,
the continuous circles that cry
and come ashore amid blood.

Preferring flowers,
wild or cultivated,
I dab at weathers,
at careworn clouds.

Preferring flowers,
it is hard for me to fathom
the waves, their salt, their cunning,
the shores they determine and unfreeze.

Preferring flowers,
the sky unsettles me.

I prefer flowers
and the earth's monotony,
a life kept well within earshot of leaves.

But far out at sea
the future of flowers is planned,
themes of flowering
are rooted in the horizon.

I stand by the faggots of firewood
stacked in the yard by the door
but where in the world am I?

Am I beyond flowers,
here where the flames are born
in a shock of animal odours?

Must I acknowledge flame,
the molten, the furnace?
Recant those petals, blooms,
the softer fragrance?

Prayer

In the margin of the book
I sketch leaves, snowflakes.
This white page is a sleepiness
I want to awaken, but it is hard,
I dream only of wakefulness,
my inklings do not take hold.
Windows, mirrors, doors,
all openings like these distract me.
Hankering after order,
I remain haphazard,
charmed, enchanted by rumours.

Outside, the snow is not distracted.
It falls, intent on ending the thaw.
The grass disappears amid creases of snow
It is, I suppose, disguised against its will…
And watching the winter settle,
I imagine myself in a rowing-boat,
the shore stretching back
into the sweetness of the past
as I embark across unfrozen waters.
I'm going somewhere unknown, untroubled,
mist rises from the kindly waters,
enfolds me in its secret placid linen.

The Gift

You don't want it?
It is too wayward?

Has too many double meanings?
Smells of a burning?

Rejection is your first thought,
no need for it, you say,
erase it, destroy it.

But be warned.
Its fragments will ache like utter distance.

These snakes are not harmless.
Those ladders lead somewhere.

Now the antiquities arrive,
with their cloudless apparatus.

Let them in oh let them in.

Ashes, Eggs

A phoenix the colour of blood
and the colour of leaves
rises again from the ashes.

Here are the wings.
Here is the new shadow.
Here are the bones.
Here is the new egg.

In some rooms, the egg
will grow to flesh and birth.
In others, to song alone.

In my room, I call up the creature.
Slipshod and wet, it may come to me
or go another way.
I can compel nothing.

Come, I say, come little life,
out of the ashes, out of the egg,
come and settle here,
you phoenix of women.

The Child-stealer

Gossip, pure gossip,
words to be sewn on tight.

Behind the door,
a phlegm of yearning and terror.

A line of victims, waiting.

Out fall the babies.

Late at night, doors and windows
fly open to let her in,
Lilith, the child-stealer.

Gossip, only gossip.
Afraid of the ache?
It goes deep.And who dares to be
where that ache lives,
is born among strangers?

Out fall the babies.
Out of the pattern.
Out of the circle.
Lost forever.

Out of the light:
Out of the mirrors.

Into the dark.
Lost forever.

They fall out of the women
on to the trembling pavement.

Why?
Blood rushes away with the answer.

Mother and Child

My heart sharpened to a point
and piercing you,
my child,
who came when I called,
in the moonlight, years past,
in the little bedroom,
in the whiteness of the full moon –
I knew your sex, your name:
the prophesying was easy.
Time has brought us onward,
in its own sweet and hard way.

And my anger pierces you,
and transfixed, you watch me,
on your guard –
I pull back my weapon,
my sharpened heart pierces itself
and frees you,
and you bound away,
singing one of your own wild unique songs.

The Children

In the boundless afternoon
the children are walking
with their gentle grammar on their lips.

From door to door
the little ones go, brightly tranquil,
repenting nothing.

How safe their journey,
their placid marching,
famous and simple voyage.

Whisper to me as if I were a child
and the answer you get
let it be your oracle and mine.

Panics may still trouble us,
the archaeology of our own past,
but we are pursuing that too-knowing adult dark
with the fires and lamps of innocence.

Soon our message will reach you, our gospel.
Free at last, happy at last,
we have gone away into the wise world of the children.

The Lion from Rio

(1986)

The Hell-bender

It is an hour without heroes in an Ohio valley.

The hell-bender is there,
'a large aquatic salamander
about eighteen inches long and very tenacious of life'.

He is a summer beast
nimbly folding the water into shapes
that suit him,
his garments he might sleep or hunt in.
All feebler things are his serfs, his fodder.

(Your sigh glitters like sun on rapid glassy water,
in the valley the campers deliberate over maps;
the morning trembles in its hurt.)

The salamander pours himself through his waterfall prairies;
garden pools do not admit him
but anyway he, supple stone of blood, fiery rope,
streaks away from their logic,
away from the white proud superstitious flowers,
away from the hooded lips of the snapdragon.

He does not recognise his children
but shoots tumultuously through the water
as if his sister were with him.
He is the serpent of sun who lives in water,
he is a master of water and fire, cool heaven and hot hell;

He is clarified to his length, his spare eloquence.
He knows he will never die.
(Who said he is only a kind of fish?)
He darts through water like thread through a fine needle eye,
he is very tenacious of life.
He can bend hell.

Snake

Snake lazing in the wet grass,
less useful than cow or horse.

Line of silver on the family path,
silver as the Rio de la Plata.

Serpent silver as my ring, my bracelet,
laughing silently as those two circles.

Serpent tingling from place to place,
one of those who do not save lives,

at whom the countrywomen fling sharp stones,
but whose daughters greet with sudden smiles.

Creature more magic than mouse or rat,
more thoughtful than donkey or cat,

whose cry is mistaken for wind in the trees,
from whom so much has been stripped,

now you are only one limb,
one skein, one thumb,

you are a long thin silver skin,
a rod that works for god.

Because of your perfection
we say you possess venom and deceit

but whoever has perfection
can do without compassion.

Silver female with your nest of pure white eggs,
you live both by basking and gliding,

you die without screaming,
you come to an end,

your silver stiffening to pewter,
then thawing back into the shallows of earth.

Your young wriggle free,
bruised but seamless,
each one her own stepping stone.

The Vision of the Blessed Gabriele
Carlo Crivelli, National Gallery, London

In the evening sky, swallows

and the saint in his robes of evening cloth
gazing upward with his worried stare.

Is it because there is no star?

His feet have slipped out of their sturdy medieval scholl sandals.
He kneels on hard sand where thin grasses fountain
and starfishy cacti flourish near a few egg-shaped pebbles.

The frail tree that for years has borne no plums
touches both the saint's shoulder and the sky.
He is holding his hands palm to palm,
making the old holy arch of fingers and thumbs,
his two little fingers making an exact oval.

He looks up at her as if she's a trespasser,
hanging there in her larger oval in the sky,
the queen and her babe,
as if he sees her as the queen of untruthfulness.

How worried and angrily he stares at her,
his hands kept holy and invulnerable,
his bare feet ugly and ordinary, a man's feet
on a man's earth,
behind him the barren tree
and above him, she and her fertility.

Swags of fat fruit, unbelievable ripeness, loll across the sky
supported by an old ragged linen hammock;
hanging from the sky not stars but outsize heavenly fruit
knotted in a casual arrangement of dirty bandages.

On the sandy ground his holy book lies open,
forgotten, its script of red and black abandoned
as in horror he stares up at the fruit,
apples and pears from a giant's orchard.

Who put them there, apple and pear,
growing on the same branch, fruit bigger than a child's head?

The hedgehoggy halo of the saint quivers.

Within this glistening vagina the sky has blurted open
like an eye or a fruit, there is this queen or golden doll
carrying her stiff golden child,
golden and ruby-red couple in the sky,
cargo lugged along by cherubs, the crumpled robe
of the woman evidence of their haste.
They peer round the edges of the mandorla, singing a suitable song.

And like a gulliver the helmeted man
with his thoughtful grieving head
lies face down on the path in the wood,
alive or dead, who knows?

Not the saint, still staring up at the sky with its storm of fruit,
at the mother of gold, her foot set on fruit,
on another goddess's golden apple.
The child holds either a second golden apple or maybe a golden ball.

The saint gapes. This is the pain of the answered prayer.

In the pond by Gabriele's feet, in the green water,
the drake moves to the lustrous duck
with almost unnoticed longing, with vigilant love.

On the branch of the plum tree, a bird is about to fly away,
north to China or south to India.
When the bird has flown the saint will be able to weep.

The Weather House
(for Peter)

I usually understand you
when you are working with electricity
because we have often run away together
into the park of storms
where the thunder and his sister lightning live;
there the clouds come to us like pets,
eligible grey mammoths asking to be fed and groomed.
We build our weather house
from the shaking white boughs of electricity;
the branching sky alive with the sleepless storm
is our garden where we gather flowers of fire and hail.
When we fear our life is slipping
back into familiarity and calm ground
we return to the special house with its trembling galvanic rooms,
to the garden seared with the tallness of trees,
to ardent air prickly with hope of rain.
How the clouds crush us under huge pigeon-grey feet
before releasing their naked furnaces of rain on us,
till we are like fountains kissing!
How the storm aches with its own fame, its long steps
pouncing to reach us!
Electricity wires us, it shoots its fix into our veins
and our dreams lengthen into flooding weather, the sweet breath
of downpour, the waterfall gasp of it.
I usually understand you
when you are working with electricity
and despite the shocks
I clasp you in my arms, our skins jolting with the power,
sharing the voltage,
Storm the friend and lover of our hearts.

Selena

'her cherry's in sherry' – WOMAN'S PERIOD

The unripe cherry has the luxurious bitterness
of the earth's satellite, the scarlet morals of it,
its acid blotches stinging your tongue;
a moon cherry that mulishly leaves its flavour
in your mouth all month; and that secret early woman
in the sky, whose soft authority will not fly away
but who holds us in her strong birthmarked arms,
or hides us behind her natural naive skirts; that taste
of sharp cherries steeping our tongues only means
we are her namesakes, the selenas...

She is the poverty of an unimportant person,
a boy, say, or a simpleton, one grown but not
and never to be adult;
she may be persistent as a child that sucketh long,
or as reproachful as headmistress; her green-goose
ceilings and her books of grief are all her;
on these observatory nights when the taste of oboes
blots out what you said or might have said to me,
she falls in scalding rain, she approaches the waning sea,
accepting without protest her unprotected position.

She stands before us, a sudden window, an intense door;
though she lets nothing ever be quite closed or quite open.
There is always one more letter to be learned
in her alphabet, one next fruit to be tasted;
after the sour text of the cherry, the golden and tiring orange,
the juicy pang of the scarce pear, the pearly apple's
pedestrian-calm;
the clingstone peach with pink and velvety skin;
her hands offer a midnight feast, her bride's charm.
She is almost capsizing with the fruit she brings.

All her roamings lead her to richness,
a richness that, as soon as it's at its height,
begins to diminish, little by little, until it becomes
another currency, another night's work in a sky so intimate
it reaches the most sensitive part of the world, a leaf maybe,

or a fish sleepless in his ocean,
or a pillow-slip blowing in the wind that has waited an eternity on the line
for this touch of moonlight on the worn white tucks and embossings of its linen,
selena's touch, her concubine's breath,
her fruits and their felicity.

Disdainful Jack

After the painting Our Jack *by Henry Scott Tuke, depicting Falmouth-born*
Jack Rolling on the quay punt Lily, *off Custom House Quay, 1886*

The boy in the bright blue coat,
navy-blue cap jammed on cropped head,
right hand hooked loosely in the rigging,
boy with his sad monastic look,
his uncomplaining expectant stare,
his knowledge of blue.

Behind him, over his shoulder,
rises the terraced harbour town,
its royalist church and roughcast houses.
Its unsheltering streets
only numb or vex him.
He has no time for the land, nor it for him.
Ashore, he trips facetious in clogs,
but on deck his feet are light and undisabled.

With little humour and less hope,
he stares disdainfully at the painter, at us.
He dwells on the voyages he's chosen,
the hammock he'll be suspended in,
the little whips of salt already burning his lungs.

He has no time for luck.
His look tells us that, plainly.
He watches the waves,
his eye forming its own past tense,
looking beyond Tuke
far out to sea,
to the day or night of his drowning.

In blue jacket and blue hat,
dressed for sea and sky,
Jack's at a standstill, lounging stiffly,
prisoner of his own dignity.

He has no sweetheart.
He keeps his energy for knowing the sea.
His gaze is the narrow ledge along which he inches his way,
lonely but used to it, to the narrowness,
the fear of missing his step.

How the ocean will welcome Jack,
who knows the cues of the drama,
who appreciates the cabaret of storm,
the syncopation of the tides.

Only when the waves close over his head
will he smile, relax, at last open his heart,
find his expected home, his unexpected happiness.

Wise sailor, he never learned to swim
and so can sink without a struggle,
the fraternal waves letting him down gently .
on the rope of his last breaths,
Jack safe forever now
in one of the galleries of the sea.

Horse of the Month

Here is a horse made of sleeplessness.
He is devoted to me.
I am sewn to his saddle,
am his established rider.

Breathing upon the sky,
the horse makes me love him.
He repeats his breath of flame.
The sky is burning, old shawl.

The trash and dust of smoke
is luck on our tongues.
The horse begins to speak, composedly.
We ride down green lanes, clover byways.

I ride him like jewels,
We wheel around our red-coral valley,
inseparable, sleepless,
grass turning to fire wherever our hooves of blood fall.

Orion

Orion standing at ease
just above the horizon.

Offer the dreamer
a window
through which she may see
the most secret parts
of the warrior.

Orion,
the within-er,
the penetrator.

The god's cool semen
falls upon her,
he throws it upon her
as if flinging
the last drops of wine from his cup.

Her dream will come true.
A child is waiting for its life.

The thunder-lord of stars is wailing,
changeling caught by flesh again.

Giving Birth

Delivering this gift
requires blood,
a remote room,
the presence of overseers.

They tug a child
out of the ruins of your flesh.

Birth is not given.
It is what is taken from you;
not a gift you give
but a tax levied on you.

Not a gift but a bout
that ages both the contestants.

Birthshocks hold on tight, for years,
like hooked bristles of goosegrass,
cleavers clinging to your skirt and sleeves.

The raw mime of labour
is never healed,
in giving birth
the woman's innocence goes,
loss you can't brush away,
it stains all your new clothes.

No longer can you be half-woman, half-bird.
Now you are all woman,
you are all given away,
your child has the wings,
can resist the pull of the earth.

You watch her rush up,
clowning her way through the cloud.

And you applaud.

Chrysalis

Like all mothers
I gave birth to a beautiful child.
Like all mothers
I wiped myself out,
vanished from the scene
to be replaced by a calm practical robot,
who took my face,
used my bones and blood
as the framework
over which to secure
her carapace of steel, silicon and plastic.
I was locked out of her clean carpentry
and smoothly-reprimanding metal.

Yet that robot's rude heart
flowed with love's essential fuel
because my child was one of the millions
of beautiful children
and knew how to tackle the machine.
She embraced the robot woman lovingly
each day
until her circuits and plastics wore away.
Now the soft real skin can grow,
the blood and breath move again,
the android is banished.

I emerge from the chrysalis
and go forward with my child
into the warm waters of the sea
in which we are both born at last,
laughing, undamaged,
bathing alive in this salty blue,
my motherhood born out of her,
her woman's name and noon out of me.

Child and Toy Bear

It is essential
to have the bear
in the bed
though he is nameless
and disregarded throughout the day.
At night he must lie beside her
so that she can sleep,
his black nose firmly clenched
in her hand,
the spar that keeps her afloat all night.

Miss Butterfly, Miss Moth

Butterfly and moth,
one primrose pale,
the second grey as god himself,
both dead,
the child keeps them
in a Flora carton
with air-holes pierced in it;
airy tomb,
plastic sepulchre
she has given to moth and butterfly
as a sanctuary
where they can find peace,
transform to their next stage
which, she sings hopefully,
(Miss Butterfly, Miss Moth),
will be fairy or elf
but fears will be only wing-tip dust,
a tick of mist;

for the child has undreamed her song before.

Bear-hug

Childlessness crushed me,
a bear-hug

I never breathed
till I bore her

though now in her clasp
I hurt

being drawn so far
from my breathless life

Why compose
on a guitar
at six years old
a curious refrain
entitled
Horse Mane?

But she does

The Child

1

Elaborate manifestation of a smiling dog
clockworking his way over the carpet;
he crouches and barks in a high peeping metallic woof;
the child follows the toy into the room,
remarking calmly, he's really a hedgehog, you know…

2

The wind windowed me out
but I held on to my friend
or my friend held me with his teeth.

Did it hurt, I ask.
No, she says, it didn't.
Landing safe in the net of her dream.

3

Or she dreams of the cat,
his dovetail pleasures.

She dreams I was angry with her.

She dreams she had an egg
which hatched out into a nasty chick.

She dreams she was given another egg
And all the other children had eggs too.

4

Another dream (she said)
was when I had a little cat
that got smaller and smaller
and ran into the bush;
when I called it
lots and lots of little dogs came out.
Sober dream dogs,
gentle canine companions.
In the child's dream they bark quietly.

5

As soon as she wakes
she starts up all her unmarried nonsense.
The rebellious parents
have to find all she needs,
her props;
they puff up and down stairs,
supplying dolls, pearls, frogs, rice, birds.

To the child nothing is a luxury,
every thing is a necessity.
For her, each day has the glamour of convalescence,
all conversations possess the repartee of scripture.

Masks

The child has masks.
It is easy to forget this.
Behind her masks
of today and tomorrow
is yesterday's face,
see, she is still too young
to understand anything
but food and sleep.
My threats are no way
to break her silences,
to curb her fires,
there must be a way
of speaking
that runs true and clear
from the womb's infant
to the child who faces the world,
her school masks of fear and pride
sprouting fresh each day;
she flinches but does not retreat;
she wears a bruised lazy-mask,
a stiff oldfashioned anger-mask,
one summer mask glitters, gifted with speech,
another is a poke-tongue laughter mask.
She has her heroic silver bedtime mask.
My own pedantic mother-mask watches.

There must be a language
for me to speak, for her to utter;
a language where the sweet and the bitter
meet; and our masks melt,
our faces peep out unhurt, quaint and partial as babies.

Act of Love

At night, riding our bed like a willing and dethroned horse,
we are secret depositors proud of our flaws,
flaws that scratch a diamond;
you are a stinging mirror to me, I another to you.
We are each a bird ruthless as cat
but we let that cruelty go into the dark
and lie lithe as lizards, side by side,
our fingernails extracting silver from our hearts,
the distinctive lode we work,
darkness arcing with our buck and doe brights
until we rest for a little, partners slumped on the ropes of night's ring.

Our outstretched arms anchor us, inseparable;
my nipple is hard as diamond, treble and desirous;
my breast-skin soft as unchaperoned moss;
your hand on it a serious shimmer;
my breast grows newer, newer,
my yanked-open laceless nightgown's bodice,
its cotton seam is caught tight around my ribs
where my heart is beating gravely and loudly,
its blood full of steadfast strength and mystery.

The night outside is a teetotal drum we flood into silence
as your delicate hard sex presses against my hip;
when we meet and join we hold our breath,
then breathe out all the burning novelty of our bodies,
a big vapour furling into the room, flag
made from our clear-sky flesh, our unearthly diplomacy,
our hauntingly-real fuck;
I watch my familiar but elaborately-lifted leg
misty and incredulous in the straight-faced dark.

And as we are not blind or dumb
this is the time we stare and cry out best
as we wear out our weariness with thrusting,
our eyes open and glossy, our throats humble with aahs,
sighing into inaudibility, our lips soft reams
of silence; we're giddy with our tongues' work,
as if two serpents had become brother and sister...

As we cast ourselves into the night and the act,
our smooth knuckles shine,
we are gasping as we smell the sleep to come,
waiting for us beyond this untraceable room;
now we clamber the summit of old-friend mountain,
rising faster in our clamour,
swinging locked-together in our bell-apple nakedness,
in the double-pink hammock of the night
made of touch and breath,
(the purposes of the engineering!),
a labour of love as we rush towards that trembling edge,
toppling over yelling into the fall, the rapids,
the waters we enter, fluid as them,
my sex hot and hidden, perfect and full,
the corner of our sinews turned,
a clear answer found, its affirmative leaping from our mouths,
my body's soft freight shaking and accepting
in the clairvoyance of orgasm,
and your answering sheer plunge from mountaintop
into river,
flowing where the bed was.

Sleep takes us then and drops us into its diocese,
drops us from night's peak into a dawn
of martial ardour, of trees mad
with old-clothes spite, a morning
where the starving still wait for us,
each with their lonely cloudy gaze.

So only the sugars of the night offer us any breakfast,
only our night's act of love feeds us,
the remembrance of our bodies like slow-moving turtles
lifted from the sweetness of a sea of honey,
flying into more sweetness.
Only the touchwood of our sweet bed
dams the savage sour torrent of the day.

In the morning we must say goodbye, not hello,
goodbye until the untouchable day has gone
and the night recalls us again to our study,
to our sweating gypsy-wagon sheets,
our navaho pillows and rich pastures,
the mintage of our wild skins.

The Martyrdom of St Polycarp

He had known John
and others who had known the Lord
but he was betrayed by a servant,

arrested late in the evening
at a farm outside Smyrna,
hens scattering in panic,
geese retreating angrily,
children peeping from corners
to find out who are heroes,
who are villains.

This happens around the year 155,
the arrest of an old man
who had known those who had known
the Lord,
had known John.

In the city
a crowd assembles for the games,
officials, wives, magnates, courtesans,
labourers, idlers, children, artisans;
animals baying, trumpeting,
the stench not a clean farmyard stench
but a festering stink,
the reek of a blood circus.

The old man and the proconsul converse,
they see eye to eye,
they are the only philosophers
within five hundred miles,
and able to bear their differences,
the roman reluctant
to condemn the venerable man
whose honour he can see.

The old man shrugs, smiles.

'How can I curse Christ,
for in all my eighty-six years
I have never known him do me wrong...'

And the crowd is yelling,
                              'Kill him,
he is the one who destroys our gods...'

Even the cripples and lepers join in.

The circus gods need blood or ashes.
So because he is commanded
the proconsul orders the burning of Polycarp

'and the flames made a sort of arch,
like a ship's sail
filled with the wind,
and they were like a wall round the martyr's body;
and he looked, not like burning flesh,
but like bread in the oven
or gold and silver being refined in the furnace.'

He was like bread in the oven!
Like gold or silver in the furnace!

He turned the torture circus
to a fiery circus of joy, flames of the spirit.

But the cruel spectators did not clap their hands,
or fall to their knees, or say to the children,
look, there is a miracle, a man alive in the flames.

Did the people say, have our gods done such thing

Did they warm themselves at those flames?

The old man stood
with the flames flowing round him
like a weir of fire,
sailing in his ship of fire,
safe in his tent of flames
as the outraged crowd damned him.

At a sign from the proconsul
(curious in private life
about the supernatural)
a bored boy-executioner
braves the miraculous ark of flame,
pierces the old man's heart,
freeing Polycarp,
who kicks his corpse aside
and becomes a soul
and the crowd go on cheering,
children laughing, the rubbish gods ungrieving.

Hide and Seek

The child might be hiding in the ship
or in the cave,
or in the garden where the morning-glory
will find him some pretty name;
he might be hiding in the tree
whose shed needles fall like quills
on to the pitch of the dry lawn;
he might hide in a tower
built by a father for a son who never appeared,
the son dreamed-of but never caught up
into the real photographs of life;
the boy might hide by the cat-happy door,
or find some waterfall behind which to shelter,
be shuttered-in by the sheer fall of water;
he must hide somewhere.
He is a virtual prisoner in the powerhouse of the page,
must hide from the words thumping and beating on his head,
but where shall he hide, this boy who has not yet learnt
how to talk like a child,
or discovered that an evasive answer is the best way
to get uninterrupted possession of your day?
He hides everywhere, primitive, prodigal,
playing any number of odd games
in the garden of the red-eyed fish, their pool of stone and weed,

or in the stables where three horses watch him,
startled but, like electricity at rest, intensely patient.
The child hides, underfed in his blue shirt and french trousers,
in the room where I expected to find anyone else but him,
even a flock of those glossy and black gregarious birds
or the stately golden sane old dog of our crazy neighbours;
butter-finger room I at once let slip away into dullness,
losing him, he is not even behind those rivals, the curtains.
The child hid in a ship
and sailed away over an ocean, beneath deep-sea stars,
into the tenderness of storms,
the tempests, the burning calms,
the retentive and temperamental weather of a child
for whom no reward was offered and to whom nothing was promised.

The Lion from Rio

Golden inclination
of the huge maned head
as he rests against my knee,
his massiveness like feathers against me
amid this Rio crowd
through which he came to me,
this lion, my lion,
my lion of lifelong light,
padding unnoticed through the carnival.
Now his beast head rests in my lap,
golden flood, I am laden with it.
Looking up at me with his gentle puzzled gaze,
he says helplessly, but I am a man, a man!

My own child could have told me.
He was a man.
How could I not have seen it?
Listen again, he is drowsily moaning,
I am a man.

August Boy

The forest of summer is its own weight in gold
and you have climbed the tallest tree at noon
to bask above me and to kiss heaven, the fiery alpine.
High spirits! Silent golden child,
odd smiling pondering boy blossoming in a tree,
what country have you left to come and dwell here
in the burning branches and lion breath of the woods?
Child, boy, son I shall not carry, bear or nourish,
glowing ghost, summer boy who beckons to me
as I stand watching, soles of my feet scorching on the sandy path,
I know you are not a child I can claim,
you are not a child of the flesh, the fierceness of that.
Child without questions, child vigilant in a tree,
amazing as any thing made of gold, you live where the future is,
with all its carelessness and charm, its mistrust of direct answers.
The summer will not leave you behind, you are where summer is,
you are the heart of its heart, riding your solar beast,
the thoroughbred summer.
When I ask you your name you smile and say, 'you know my name'.
Furnace-Page of the Green and Gold of August,
Seigneur of the Summer, young Caesar of the Blazing Leaves,
wild, lenient and motherless, I recognise your boyish title,
Eagerly, easily, I lose my heart to you, my Heatwave Cupid.

Adventures with My Horse

(1988)

Jungian Cows

In Switzerland, the people call their cows
Venus, Eve, Salome, or Fraulein Alberta,
beautiful names
to yodel across the pastures at Bollingen.

If the woman is busy with child or book,
the farmer wears his wife's skirt
to milk the most sensitive cows.

When the electric milking-machine arrives,
the stalled cows rebel and sulk
for the woman's impatient skilful fingers
on their blowzy tough rosy udders,
will not give their milk;

so the man who works the machine
dons cotton skirt, all floral delicate flounces
to hide his denim overalls and big old muddy boots,
he fastens the cool soft folds carefully,
wraps his head in his sweetheart's sunday-best fringed scarf,
and walks smelling feminine and shy among the cows,

till the milk spurts, hot, slippery and steamy
into the churns,
Venus, Salome, Eve, and Fraulein Alberta,
lowing, half-asleep,
accepting the disguised man as an echo of the woman,
their breath smelling of green, of milk's sweet traditional climax.

Killiow Pigs

from Killiow Country Park, near Truro

Five adolescent suckling pigs
fanned out alongside their sleeping mamma;
each daughter big as an alsatian dog,
her five petticoat-pink starch-skinned girls.
They sleep with resolution and vitality.
Our admiration does not wake them.
Fed on apples, their flesh is ready-seasoned.
This afternoon heap of pig breathes a clean dusk
into the air; spring and dung,
rhododendrons, sour vapour of swill and straw.
With their sexy squiggle tails,
their ears soft as cats but big and lopped-over
like ambitious rabbits, with their long carefree
strokeable backs, their feet comic and smooth,
snouts succulent,
these sisters lie outspread, five cordial orchids
against mother's blushing pungent bulk,
dreaming of orchards
where an exiled male roots and roams,
his boar thighs tough and angelic,
his head lowered to the cool brisk echoes of morning,
his ringed nose a gleam of gravity,
his sudden stillness all swinish magnetism.
Dossing mother and daughters quiver in sleep,
the juice of desire lolloping over their lips;
snouts swell with love; tails uncurl, grow fine
and tender as silk;
each meets her orchard lover,
dreamy pigs in their matrilineal slumber.

As we watch these females, hope and desire
rise in us, a cloud of matrimonial heat,
blossoming and getting the better of us,
oh these shameless porcine arrangers of marriages!

Alice

I live in one room.
My bedroom is my kitchen,
my study is my bathroom.
I am absorbed by my own powers,
feeling beautiful and resourceful.
I am awaiting an avalanche of young.
In me fifteen new hearts beat.
My stretched belly-skin is near splitting,
my bulk is pastoral, I know.
I smell of melons and cheese.
I am not restless or nervous.
I look pityingly at you
who don't possess my one room.
Soon there will be such a squall of piglet,
a shoal of tails and tingling ears,
an april fall of flesh,
a sixty-legged blind creature,
not a scratch on it;
a chute of pig, shriller than puppies,
fitter than fleas. I know all this
from previous experience.
Every one of my imminent litter will possess
our breed's gift for caricature.
The dog will turn and run from their chaos.
They will not be dangerous in their cherry-pale
and sugar-bright skins; but loud.
In the paddock they will race and scamper.
Like mine, their lives will be immensely public.
Under the afternoon sky they will sleep
as babyishly as in any cartoon
that would bonnet and bib them,
as if their flesh were lifelong safe, inedible,
and myself, Alice, their mother,
a human mother resting with full breasts bared
and aching in the flickering shade of the mimosa tree.

Alice's Husband

He is both predictable and unpredictable.
Both gracious and fierce, heroic
and brutal, a gothic husband.
Just when I have forgotten him, he returns,
savage and hopeful, pale both with lust
and with an aesthete's melancholy. This
was not necessarily his idea, he means. Elvish,
his turn of head; his glance by turns
high-souled, gloomy, flirtatious, deferential.
Glowering, he sniffs towards me. Ringed,
his snout is merely embellished, not owned.
He draws my smell into his nostrils
with a shudder of scandalised disbelief,
then trots a little closer; all this
surveillance! He moves forward, he who
has no after-life. His back is long,
his thighs huggable, his tail a perfect solo,
his odour of honey, pepper, camomile and wax,
a reek of desire, my infinite temptation, his bait,
this fallen angel of the pigs.
His testes are charming, burly,
they billow out, ballooning
from sudden excess of emotion; his plum-coloured
tongue lolls.
His powerful torso is like the beginning of flesh,
his massive capable jaws good as any dog's;
distract him from me now
and he'll charge you, speed and force, for the kill.
He is the axe at my root. His weight on me
is aficionado, apostle, family-man,
a giant refreshed.

God Dividing Light from Darkness

Michelangelo

An old man,
a feeble agèd grumpy
grimacing old god in the clouds,
cloud-bearded, lear-haired,
clambering through womb-mist,
fumbling, lost, tunnelling
through epiphanic coils,
their foams and jades and grimes,
their hulled and frilled scapes.

As old as these nesting clouds
that water-lily the void together,
he throws up his fog-robed arm
and delivers the world;
out of the womb-age of the old god
comes a cloud of earth and sea,
sky and dream,
ripple of sand and ripeness of rock,
fissure, passage and cave,
leaf and coriander seed,
swamp and hedgehog, etcetera...

He bears this child of his old age
without tenderness,
enraged, his heart closing
like a book of stone,
his eyes changing colour each instant,
flickering kaleidoscopic lightning;
his robes radiant waves
of cold-rainbows,
this frowning merciless old father,
minus cherubim,
bristling with opposites, the pangs of creation,
the light his perfect son,
the dark already too bad to be named,
serpent turning and grinning,
prodigal on the balance-scale.

Snakes and Quakes

Anything that wriggles
might be a snake.

Our yard grass whispers
serpentine, stern; seeding
into neighbours' neat gardens.

Coil of cloud returning
with rattling-tail;

the rain a green viper
withdrawing from life,
reclusive in the water table.

Around the new moon,
a snake of light
shakes and

the air cracks its whip;
window glass shatters;
buildings shake and boom.

The snake opens his eye.

Houses, ready to fall,
exhale the scent of him,
that breath of earth.

I sip water,
fearing everything but the snake.

I hold him,
spin in woman circles with him;
his hard dry lip against mine,
his tongue mustard,
colour and taste.

He sips my breath.

Doors move suddenly
with no help from hands;
the sky galloping,
rivers zigzagging,
the air's soft growl rippling.

Plumes of trees twist,
green and baffled.

But the serpent is already back
in his secret corner of thin air,
long-necked and unanswerable.

The earth locks its stable doors again.
The horse of quake gone.

I, snake-collared, yawning, garlanded
and sashed with serpents
invisible but coiling and scolloping
electric eelishness around me,
watch the golden worm of lightning (my beloved!)
fork his brazen tongue over the black sky,
lisping flame, stammering fire.

Thief

He will steal it, whatever you possess.
Whatever you value, what bears your name,
everything you call 'mine', he will steal.
Everything you have is frail and will be stolen from you.
Not just watch or bracelet, ring or coat,
bright objects, soft splendours, gifts, necessities,
but the joy that bends you easily and makes you feel safe,
your love of what you see each different morning
through your window, the ordinary seen as heavenly.
Your child's power, your lover's touch, will be stolen
from under your nose. He will steal everything.
He will take everything from you. You will never see him.
You will never hear him. You will never smell him.
But he will destroy you.
No surveillance is close enough, no guard clever enough,
no lock secure enough, no luck good enough;

the thief is there and gone before you have sense
of breath to cry out.
He has robbed you before, a hundred times.
You have never seen him but you know him.
You know his vermin smell without smelling him,
you know his smile of learning without seeing it,
you feel his shadow like deprival weather, grey, oppressive
You know he watches from far away or from just round the corner
as you regather your little hoard of riches, your modest share
of the world, he watches as you build your shelter of life,
your hands raw from working day and night, a house
built out of bricks that must be guessed at, groped for,
loved, wept into being; and then upon those walls
you and your people raise a roof of joy and pain, and you live
in your house with all your ordinary treasures,
your pots and pans, your weaned child, your cat and caged bird,
your soft bestiary hours of love,
your books opening on fiery pages your nights full
with dreams of a road leading to the red horses of Egypt,
of the forest like a perfumed pampered room wet with solitude.
You forget the thief. You forget his vanity,
his sips and spoonfuls of greed. But he watches you,
sly in the vaults of his wealth.
Shameless, sleepless, he watches you.
Grinning, he admires your sense of safety.
He loves all that you love.
Then, in disguise, with empty pockets, his fingers dirty
and bare rings of white skin in place of gold bands,
he comes like a pauper on a dark patchwork morning
when summer is turning round and robs you blind.
He takes everything.
He is the thief in whose gossamer trap you have been floating
all these years. He comes and takes everything.
Your house is empty and means nothing, the roof falls in
and the walls of love dissolve, made of ice;
the windows no longer watch out over heaven, the bare wooden
floors show their scars again and ache for the forest.
He takes everything you have, this thief, but gives you one gift.

Each morning you open your eyes jealous as hunger, you walk
serpent-necked and dwarf-leggèd in the thief's distorting mirrors,
you go nakedly through the skyless moonless gardens and pagodas
of envy that he gives you, the thief's gift, your seeding wilderness.

Draco, the Dreaming Snake

Like a sigh in silence, the serpent,
oh, he dreams me, in his solar, in his naked house.

The serpent weeps if he thinks he is not wanted.
But he is. He dreams me. In his solar.
In his room for sun. In his pond of light.

Oh his great energy and his cleverness,
out of the naked house of the virgin he creeps,
skill and shame mixed in him,
and a vapour about his skin I shiver for,

glimpsing how it works, his magic,
but only a glimpse, he is all his own magician,
he sleeps as he travels over the clays and granites

of the land, never unemployed, always a worker,
yes, he gathers up the whirlwind of the sleepless
and finds some sleep for them. That is his work.
He dreams me. My serpent dreams me.

It is his intimidating but helpless gift.
In a fountain of pure undwindling water he dreams me,
he dreams me in the soft male heart of the lily,
its innocent roar.

He dreams me in my dream of the paper dead, the lost parents.
He dreams the shadow that does the washing-up
and the ironing in the new house. He dreams Mother Lion.

He dreams he is a serpent
who will be the last one of us all to die.
He dreams that all he wishes for will come true.
He dreams me.

In my hand I hold a golden coin covered with blood,
He dreams this.
He dreams this baby under the blue flower of my heart.

He dreams the fragmental stealth of my spirit.
He dreams my future, he dreams my past.
He dreams the breath of this bare room,
the chimney's old ache of blackened brick,
the ceiling a caul of faded paint,
the walls objecting to windows on principle,
doors opening and closing in an ardent future,
causing horror, fear, delight,
and all these dreams move in me like sex,
with little or no punishment or revenge.

Such is the serpent's business,
making something already beautiful even more possible,
the hiss of his hope touching a nerve.

Ancient serpenting tourist, he travels the world,
naked as Celsius, naked as the great sophistication of glass,
naked as the flare of spice from your aroused skin,
naked as whatever again and again stretches its long coiled self
towards us, dreaming us and asking for our dreams.

We dream him a new skin to cocoon his aspen heart,
to clothe his whip of a spine; a perfect fit;
tender as an eyelid;
his new scales glitter like rain on his hooded head,
and he dreams us, dreaming him.

Overnight

I am pinning wet laundry on the line an hour
before summer bedtime,
my shadow in the moonshed night holds up
warm dripping, gathers, soapy scallop-edged hems,
a smocking of wrung-out blouses
shepherdessing me through my chosen task.
My rough fingers pin up his hugging shirts,
his ten long white arms fly out in spirals of spray,
the wet tails of my skirts twist to snares and nooses,

77

a daughter's near-adolescent fashions tremble and dance,
the bath towels pull like tarpaulins. I haul
them all up on the line, giving them to the moon
for drying.

I thought I was not meant to be loved,
but these wet clothes weigh me down with love,
its luscious clumsiness, its terror and wit.
I look up at the moon.
He will do his share of the work, I know,
even though he's only at half-strength;
all night he will dry the clothes with his clean clannish breath.
They will not be called strangers by him.
I leave him bending forward over the garments like a lover
and come to you.

We are beyond clothes;
naked, our bodies pillowed and spelling out breath,
we are the long kite-ribboning lovers;
my flame of orgasm is innocence returning, yours breaks
on me like a sky of connubial indoor rain.

Out in the yard, the washing sways and lulls;
solemn as children, the pale plump dresses,
the collars and cuffs with their couvades of lace,
the fledgling buttons flouncing in moonlight,
a row of fluttering sentries not needing their colours
until morning,
when I slouch sleepily out and unpeg them, creased
and armour-stiff, missing the moon, fearing bird-breath,
eggshell-bridge sky, the expectations of day;
in the house they lie like elderly rustics,
awaiting the phoenix of the iron to smooth them back to life.
Alive again, they desire and cover our family nakedness.

The Horse Who Loves Me

1

The horse who loves me is strong and unsaddled.
He desires to learn nothing.
He sleeps standing, like a tree.
He lifts dawn on his willing shoulders.

I ride the horse who loves me,
hands twined in his bashful mane,
knees gripping his nut-butter flanks.

The horse who loves me goes on tiptoe,
his hooves tap the fiery earth.
The long leisure of his muzzle pleases me.

His smell is salt and primroses, honeycomb
and furnace. Oh the sweat of his glittering tail!
How he prances studiously, the horse who loves me.

The horse who loves me has no hobby but patience.
He brings me the gift of his honesty.
His big heart beats with love.
Sometimes he openly seeks a wife. But he returns to me.

The horse who loves me is one of the poor of Paradise.
He enjoys Paradise as such a loving horse might,
quietly watching the seven wonders of the night.

2

Look at my horse!
His neatly-plaited snowy tail
hangs like a fine finger between his pearly buttocks.
His name can be Desire, or Brother.

He does not complain of my weight on his back
any more than darkness complains of its loneliness.

The horse who loves me
wields the prick of pain that caps the dart of love.
We gasp at its pang,
then race for the scaled wall of the sky.

The horse who loves me
takes me beyond the lengths grief goes to,
beyond the strides joy makes,
beyond the moon and his sister the future.

This heaven-kissing horse of mine
takes me with him to his aerial home.
Below us, roofs grey, fields fade, rivers shiver, pardoned.
I am never coming back.

from Clayman, Leatherman and Glassman

Clayman

3

He puts the broken slabs of dry tough white clay
in an old tin bath and pees on it gently
to moisten it; the best way, the old way.
Then he leaves the clay to soak and soften.

Returning, he pinches the clay, testing its pliancy.
He puts his fingers to his mouth, tasting.
The sweet odd taste like wine and raw egg and mashed swede,
its smell of mould and rain and alcohol
tell him it's ready. He adds
a fistful of ground flint, to increase the whiteness,
a pinch of calcined animal bone, to add translucence
and blessing.

He lifts the clay in both hands
and thuds it down on the wooden benchtop,
knocking it into preliminary shape
by hammering it repeatedly with his fists,
then pressing the weight of his spread hands
down on it; the air must be forced out.
He grabs the clay up, throws it down,
beats it with his fists again. He punches
and pummels it, groaning and urging himself on;

it must be done;
this is not the gentle time.

With a wire he splices the clay in two, like cheese;
examines it for air bubbles.
Walloping the two halves together with a clap of laughter,
he wedges the clay, pushing the softest clay out
in convexing folds further than the firmest seams of clay.
After much adroit pushing and pulling with his hands,
much gripping and slapping, thwacking and thumping,
thrashing and pounding, the boneless clay is ready.

4

He holds the first slab of her,
preparing to create his love from clay,
(from the female genre of mud, earth,
clay, white silt).

He looks for the first hint of her
within the mass that he belabours,
as he moulds, as he finger-carves,
as he pulls off the many veils of clay that enwrap her;
in his hands the clay is shuddering;
loiteringly, he coils, kneads, shapes, coaxes.

Sweating, he plumps the mound of white clay
to a rough torso shape; a woman;
he hugs the clay to his own breast
as he works, shaping base of throat,
rib-cage, collar-bone, breasts, waist
and slight flare of hips; the white torso
presses hard against his flat hand;
they are breast to breast.
Under his hands he feels clay, gristle, sinew.
He sets her on the table.
With fresh clay, he rolls the cylinder that will be her arms.

5

He holds a damp white boulder of clay in his hands.
It is bigger than a woman's head,
for the clay will shrink as it dries.
He places the lump of clay gently on the wooden board.

It is white and lopsided, vague, blind.
He sits a little way off, waiting to recognise her;
waiting for the clay to give him permission
to look for the woman it wants to be.
He is scared; his skills, his conviction,
his husbandry fade. His dream of making a woman
out of clay, her voice instructing him fade.

The palms of his hands flutter with energy that eludes his grip;
he dare not turn to look at the finished torso under her cloak
of sacking, nor at the perfect arms and legs lying
under similar blankets; waiting.

Why am I making this woman?
I have made her a beautiful room,
with polished floor, mirrors, flowers,
with silent curtains, a bed of fluffy satin,
raisins and chicory to eat.
Why am I making her?

Not for a sister, not for a mother.
A companion? A friend?

Like an islander alone, he needs her.
She alone can explain why he needs her.

Conclusion: Wives and Workers

These are the three workers, with their materials,
clay, leather, glass;
here are their wives, Lady Glass, Lady Black-Leather, and Lady Clay.

The men work in daylight,
they have the hands of their fathers,
the eyes and hearts of their mothers.

Clayman labours with the soft solid burden of clay.
He loves it like the ground under his feet, with ordinary
useful love. He develops his husbandry,
his hands unfaltering in the daylong odour of earth.

Above his head, the roof shines with gold
from ridge to eaves, the gilded house of the married man.

Leatherman unreels a long length of indolent tanned skin,
jetsam delicate as air. He strokes its spiced weave
like pulled-out lace from a lavish corsetry.
His blood-roots quicken and quiver like a beaten drum of feathers.
He works fast with template and broad knife; giving
leather its after-life.
It is his gift, flagrant, simple and secret.

Glassman breathes in a wisp of carbons.
Torment of glass dust hides in the mist of his lungs.
His lips murmur; incantation and joke,
incandescent forfeit.
He makes a crescent moon of wild robust glass,
letting the glass flow and shift, adaptable,
the vernacular of glass rustling.

The wives watch.

One came from the willing earth,
to live in his helpless boudoir,
under his bright sloping roof;
so that he will never be homesick.

One came from her man's love of leather;
her love is thin as sky, tough as whipcord.
His heart hangs from her wide and studded leather belt.

One came from his glass-wet dream,
his potent sigh;
her love is his one strong plank
from a wrecked ship of glass.
Over hurdles of glass, she leaps towards him.

One loves Glass and marries him.
One loves leather and marries Leather.
One loves earth and marries Clay.
There are long silent busy nuptials
in the nights;
each woman burns her own tongue in the flame of love.

Each Eva permits an Adam to create her;
so she may begin her work,
which is to finish his work for him.

Claywoman dissolves the pots and bowls in rain,
bringing them down to earth again.

Leatherwoman lets the killed leather graze,
solid from horn to hoof. The herds
look up, surprised, then feed again, big tongues
simplifying grass.

Glasswoman sets glass singing; the birds flock
and fuss; next, fruit ripens into colour, fragrance,
eloquent seed; real fish grunt through real water;
a world of glass goes free, learns life,
the weight of death.

Taxing the Rain

(1992)

Angel

The angel is coming down,
white-hot, feet-first,
abseiling down the sky.

Wingspan? At least the width
of two young men lying head to head,
James and Gary, their bare feet
modestly defiant, pointing north,
south.

The angel has ten thousand smiles,
he is coming down
smooth as a sucking of thumbs,

he is coming down on a dangle of breath,
in blazing bloodsilk robes.
See the size and dignity of his great toes!

He comes down in a steam of feathers,
a dander of plumes,
healthy as a spa,
air crackling round him.

Yes, he comes down
douce and sure-winged,
shouting sweetly through the smoke,
'J'arrive!'

Hovering on fiery foppish wings,
he gazes down at me
with crane-neck delicacy.

I turn my head from his furnace,
his drastic beauty...
he is overcoming me.

On my crouched back his breath's
a solid scorching fleece.
In my hidden eyes, the peep of him hurts.

He waits,
he will not wait long.

Flames flicker along my sleeve
of reverence as I thrust my hand
into the kiln of the seraph.

Howling, I shoulder my pain,
and tug out one feather,
tall as my daughter.

When I look up,
he's gone on headlong wings,
in a billow of smoulders,
sparks wheeling, molten heels

slouching the side wind. 'Adieu!'

Goodbye, I wave,
my arm spangled with blisters
that heal as I stare at the empty sky.

And the feather?
                    Is made of gold.
Vane and rachis, calamus
and down. For gold like an angel
joyeth in the fire.

'No pudieron seguir soñando'

'They could not go on dreaming.'

Storyteller North and Bystander South
stopped dreaming. So did East and West.

There was no more dreaming for Sun,
no more dreaming for Moon.

'No pudieron seguir soñando.'

No, they could not go on dreaming.
For all the Horses, no dreams.

For all the Mirrors, no dreams.
No dreams for the Forest,
despite his noble descent.

There is no tomorrow.
They could not go on dreaming it.

There's no tomorrow for the Mountain.
No tomorrow for the Ocean.

No dreams for the sober Whale.
No dreams for Mouse or Wolf.
No dreams for anyone.

Even the Street Women,
women of the poorer sort; they stopped dreaming.

No tomorrow for the Child
with his taste for solitude.

'No pudieron seguir soñando.'

Downhill Night and Tell-tale Dawn
stopped dreaming. So did Ghosts and Wheels.

No dreams for Globe-trotter Horizon,
no dreams for that drifter, Air.

No dreams for the Flower of Venus.

Lion stopped dreaming. Money
stopped dreaming.

All the Masks stopped dreaming.
Not one Razor or Scarecrow,
Web or Bone dreamed.

There is no tomorrow.
They could not go on dreaming it.
No.

The thinnest pane of Glass,
the most nimble and leaping Door,
the most devout Dog. No,
they could not.

Women stopped dreaming. So did Men.
'No pudieron seguir soñando.'
How could there be a tomorrow,

when none of the Trees dreamed?

When there was no dreaming for Snow,
for clannish Ant or veil-winged
Bee? Ask them to dream.

They cannot.

For even the dirty Water in the Gutter
has stopped dreaming. And not one of any
three Foxes can dream. No Thumb can dream
nor any of the Fingers of any Hand.

For there are no more tomorrows.

For the Ship cannot dream
and turns to cloud. For Cloud cannot dream
and rolls away like a stone
but it is no Stone.

The Invisible Man cannot dream.
The Seen Woman cannot dream.
Even for them, no tomorrow.

'No pudieron seguir soñando.'
They could not go on dreaming.

For the River, there's no tomorrow.
No tomorrow for the Dove,
faithful in marriage, chaste in widowhood.

Silver stops dreaming. Iron stops dreaming.
Pearls cannot dream. Nor can
Ice, Jade, Rice, Dew. No Heart
is dreaming. No Tongue is dreaming.

There is no tomorrow.
They could not go on dreaming it.

No one could.
Not even the Rain could.
Not even the Sky.

Whenever an earthquake occurs,
our planet rings like a bell;
but it has stopped dreaming.

Not one Stone in the World is dreaming.
The last word of all
is in your mouth;
slide it between my lips;
let me taste the last of salt.

Looking for Love

This woman looking for love
has to mend all the sails
that a winter of storms has ripped
to shreds, she will be sewing for years.

This guy must be looking for love.
See how he crouches like a runner
before the race.

Another man looking for love
crawls smiling up the phosphor mountains
of hell, the burning acrid slopes.

Two teenage girls speeding along
the towpath on golden-wheeled bikes,
are they looking for love?
Or are their shadows flying
over the naked Thames enough for them?

This woman looking for love
finds one tear in the rain.
If love were the remains
of a small wild horse,
or the skull of a young boy
lost in the wreck
of 'The Association',
she would have found love.

Two spitting cats
couple in the moonlit yard.
Is this love? thinks the peeping child.
She hopes not.

This woman looking for love
gets the door slammed in her face.
He's got too many wives already...

This fella looks for love
in the National Gallery,
he thinks he's Little Christ
snuggling and glittering on a Renaissance lap;
mother's boy,

whereas his wife,
rehearsing the Virtues and their Contraries,
finds love without looking,
in a room on the fourth floor of an ethereal hotel;
she doesn't ask his name.

Big Cat

A windowful of cloud.
Rain on the big sloping glass roof
falls from a once-only sky.

The lovers shiver,
their tongues spate
in their mouths
with a why and a how;
they say now, now.

The room holds them in its history,
between its pages,
as they tap at heaven.

They shake in their silver lining.

The window holds its breath.

Then the lovers come.
Then sleep purrs in their throats
like a big cat guessing names.

Trick Horse

The trick horse is a bareback horse,
a holy horse
composed of many bare backs,
many couples in union,
near-naked men and women artfully entwined,
arranged in their copulations, loins
studded together so that their balancing bodies
create the body of a horse,

a yoga of sexy reciprocations.

The reason the trick horse brings good luck?
He's made from our inclination to fuck.
Men and women grip wrists, shoulder thighs,
weave, twine, dovetail, cling, clasp
and loll; are joined in the volupté
of their disguise. All support all.

It is an act of love, however they pose.
One woman's long swoop of dark hair – horsetail.

Yet the faces of these horse-makers
are as serious as any worshippers
in more austere religions; calm copulators,
the black-moustached men gazing about in sexual
reverie; the women, in gemmed bibs,
with pearl-studded noses, are just as grave

in their abandon. Though jewels of sweat
shiver on their golden skins, they assemble
as silently and devoutly as if in church
to make this estimable shameless mount.

One woman stretching her upper body forward
to make the horse's head,
(her glossed and outspread hair the mane),
grins and raises two hennaed index-fingers
to prick up the ears
of the animal of desire and delight.

Now comes the flower-garlanded rider
of this holy horse,
a girl thumb-belled, chime-toed,
a girl naked but for flowers and bells
and gold-braided bodice,
dancing towards her mount.

Now she lowers her baton of jasmine
and bows in greeting, the many eyes
of the horse watching her,
its many musks rising and clouding about her.

One man extends his linked hands,
making a stirrup for her gilded foot,
up she vaults,
with a leaping of bells,
scaling the carnal creature,
ascending her shivery gasping horse;
she squats and kisses the topmost balancing man,
who is persevering in his desire,
sinks herself down
upon her husband-saddle,
upon the pommel
of his stiff and risen phallus,
knees gripping,
flexing her haunches
till he's deep within her yoni;
and there she sits, radiant jockey,
astride, communing
with all the members of her love horse,
who quake in complicity and delight,
then steady, willingly taking her weight.

Now the girl rider, high upon her tantrick horse,
taps its composite flanks once
with her flowery rod;
this is the trick horse that all may ride,
that all may make.

She and her companions clip clop away in rapture.

Neighbour

Holding the rain in your arms
you grow wiser, wetter!
The sky is not too big for you,
you could carry that too,
like a tree-bride or a hill-wife.
My house opens its eyes
and lets you give it tears;
how it weeps! and finds itself
next to the flooded garden.

You bring me this rain
that turns you to one
who knows the rain by heart,
whose sleeves turn to rain,
whose hands hold the rain
but as if by accident,
whose memory is now only rain,
whose future is rain,
who brings me the passions
and security of the rain.

You play the rain like a musical instrument.
Is it horn or string or percussion?
It is all. It plays, you play it,
music spills and drums, strums and hums.

As you play you observe me
with the eyes of rain,
my poorest neighbour,
my strangest friend.
You sing to me in rain,
you joke in rain,
you put rain into my arms
like flowers young as the hills.
How I hope the rain never stops,
for every inch of rain
surely is gifted
and deserves to be loved
as well as you love it.

Georgette

No matter how often she moves the furniture
she can't find her Childhood.
It is named, after the fashion of hurricanes,
Childhood Georgette.
But where is it?
No matter how often she coaxes old chairs
into new places, she can't find her Childhood.
Father grumbles quietly up and down the steps.
Mussed and sweaty,
she pushes everything back against the walls.
She looks and looks. Childhood?
Big hands clap the sky, Father is sending the rain.
She pushes her little foster bike through the rooms,
searching.
Father is at the window with his stormy thoughts.
He is shaking his branches.
Too old for a kiss? laughs Father out in the rain.
Again and again
he and the rain know what's right and what's wrong.
She leans the tear-stained bike against the wall.
Childhood?
A nudge of thunder. Don't tell lies!
She puts the furniture back how it was, everything
stares back obediently at her. Father
is muttering one of his old songs
and peeping round the door. Rain calls
out the name she never liked.
The windows don't lift a finger. Now Father
in those mirrors
is smiling at his little poupée.
Now she rides on Father's shoulders,
seeing everything, interpreting nothing.
Georgette is riding. Ice and rain on the stairs,
all the rooms galloping round and round
and hurting, Father knows where her Childhood is.

Zoo Morning

Elephants prepare to look solemn and move slowly
though all night they drank and danced, partied
and gambled, didn't act their age.

Night-scholar monkeys take off their glasses,
pack away their tomes and theses,
sighing as they get ready for yet another long day
of gibbering and gesticulating, shocking
and scandalising the punters.

Bears stop shouting their political slogans
and adopt their cute-but-not-really teddies' stance
in the concrete bear-pit.

Big cats hide their flower-presses, embroidery-frames
and watercolours;
grumbling, they try a few practise roars.
Their job is to rend the air, to devour carcasses,
to sleep-lounge at their vicious carnivorous ease.

What a life.
But none of them would give up show-business.

The snakes who are always changing,
skin after skin,
open their aged eyes and hinged jaws in welcome.

Between paddock and enclosure
we drag our unfurred young.
Our speech is over-complex, deceitful.
Our day out is not all it should be.
The kids howl, baffled.

All the animals are very good at being animals.
As usual, we are not up to being us.
Our human smells prison us.

In the insect house
the red-kneed spider dances on her eight light fantastics;
on her shelf of silence she waltzes and twirls;
joy in her hairy joints, her ruby-red eyes.

Delicious Babies

Because of spring there are babies everywhere,
sweet or sulky, irascible or full of the milk of human kindness.
Yum, yum! Delicious babies!
Babies with the soft skins of babies, cheeks
of such tit-bit pinkness, tickle-able babies, tasty babies,
mouth-watering babies.

The pads of their hands! The rounds
of their knees! Their good smells of bathtime
and new clothes and gobbled rusks!
Even their discarded nappies are worthy of them, reveal their powers.
Legions and hosts of babies! Babies bold as lions, sighing babies,
tricksy babies, omniscient babies, babies using a plain language

of reasonable demands and courteous acceptance.
Others have the habit of loud contradiction,
can empty a railway carriage (though their displeasing howls
cheer up childless women).
Look at this baby, sitting bolt upright in his buggy!
Consider his lofty unsmiling acknowledgement of our adulation,

look at the elfin golfer's hat flattering his fluffy hair!
Look next at this very smallest of babies
tightly wrapped in a foppery of blankets.
In his high promenading pram he sleeps sumptuously,
only a nose, his father's, a white bonnet and a wink
of eyelid showing.

All babies are manic-serene, all babies are mine,
all babies are edible, the boys taste best.
I feed on them, nectareous are my babies,
manna, confiture, my sweet groceries.

I smack my lips,
deep in my belly the egg ripens,
makes the windows shake,
another ovum-quake
moves earth, sky and me...

Bring me more babies! Let me have them for breakfast,
lunch and tea! Let me feast, let my honey-banquet of babies
go on forever, fresh deliveries night and day!

Faire Toad

'Foul toade hath a faire stone
in his head',
especially is this found
in the heads of old and great toads;
the fairer the stone,
the stronger his venom.

Until today I never knew
toads shed their skins; in muck and mud,
agony and triumph of transformation,
the magic of the amphibian.

Faire toad feeds only on living prey.
He carries his heart in his throat.
But for the mating time
he lives the life of a recluse.

He climbs higher and spawns deeper
than cousin frog.
When man and wife toad embrace,
they do not cease for hours
their amorous encounter.

A toad may choose to live in water or earth.
Great is his capacity for fasting.

No, he does not spit fire.
No, he does not love women,
though in stories he is royal
as any frog.
He does not suck milk from cows.

Scholar-toad sees more than we see,
his eyes are eight times
more sensitive to light
than our human clarity.
Such glooms his eyes can pierce...

My lady toad gives herself
in wax, iron, silk and wood
on the wayside altars of Central Europe.

Luck shuffles
in to the parlour which a toad visits.

If you wish for his treasure,
do not torment him or dress him
in new silk;
but give him warmth, kindness,
pleasure; then he'll be buffoon
and priest, hopping
and processing in his khaki, bronze
and sepia swarth…leave
you his jewel-head in his will,
a faire and blood-hot ruby.

Taxing the Rain

When I wake the rain's falling
and I think, as always, it's for the best,

I remember how much I love rain,
the weakest and strongest of us all;

as I listen to its yesses and no's,
I think how many men and women

would, if they could,
against all sense and nature,

tax the rain for its privileges;

make it pay for soaking our earth
and splashing all over our leaves;

pay for muddying our grass
and amusing itself with our roots.

Let rain be taxed, they say,
for riding on our rivers
and drenching our sleeves;

for loitering in our lakes
and reservoirs. Make rain pay its way.

Make it pay for lying full length
in the long straight sedate green waters

of our city canals,
and for working its way through processes

of dreamy complexity
until this too-long untaxed rain comes indoors

and touches our lips,
bringing assuagement – for rain comes

to slake all our thirsts, spurting
brusque and thrilling in hot needles,

showering on to anyone naked;
or balming our skins in the shape of scented baths.

Yes, there are many who'd like to tax the rain;
even now they whisper, it can be done, it must be done.

Building a City for Jamie

(1996)

Yule

On the tall green tree we have hung
the little golden masks of Bacchus,
the many little grins glinting and sparkling,
'oscilla ex alta suspendent mollia pinu',
waving amulets from the tall pine,
as did the roman soldiers, revering
'the cedar in its bravery',
the sacred, ever-green, ever-living pole,
recalling in winter dark that other deathless tree
whose roots are deep in little-hell,
whose highest boughs uphold great heaven.
Sweet resins fill the house,
atop the tree stands Frau Sonne, shining one...
And here on the table is our Christmas cake,
'geologically sound, with one stratum of icing,
and one of marzipan, the whole superimposed
on alluvial darkness', and 'the vast globe
of plum-pudding, the true image of the earth,
flattened at the poles', from which the flame leaps,
as it leaps along the log of yule
by whose light we watch the year's wheel turn.
Now from the popped and plundered
red and golden paper crackers, we eagerly unfold
and don our Saturnalian hats of crepe
and beneath the luminous Kissing Bough
of mistletoe and woven green bay,
we kiss in a pre-Copernican way;
the sun moves, not us, not our earth!
We beg her to live again, arise from her winter death!
All the multitude of Bacchus' golden lips
move in smiling silent supplication.
Here is your tree, here are your children, Reine Soleil,
give us your gifts...

Flood

Water asleep
all across China,

cool days and nights
of water sleeping

and growling
in its sleep,

young dog water,

and stars wanting
to be held tight,

and the rain lingual
as ever,

and China folding hands
idiomatically,

and water expatiating
and dreamy,

and not writing anything down,
and the rivers

in endless revolution,
winding in psycho-sensual economy

round and round
the scenic perfumeries,

the hills and other illuminants:

water asleep
as it circles China,

inundating the palaces,
unplanning the cities,

and floating the Buddhas
downstream in their sleep.

Tigers

My girl shivers beside me
under the quilt she sewed us all last summer.

Perhaps she dreams Freud loses all his money
in a telepathy scam

or that she attends the first performance
of Mozart's *Faust*.

She dreams she is the Tsar's favourite child,
perhaps.

Perhaps in her dream a dowry-storm of Fabergé eggs
bounces off our roof,
glittery mad jewelled hail.

I love her.
She is more like god than anyone I know.
She dreams for so long!

I never expected to paint the world
as a holy world. But I do, now.

The higher you climb, she told me,
the better the view. Don't look down.

Weeping, she dreams of women blown
to ashes, flying away,

beyond towns, bridges – they cannot get
too far away…

…even from her…

Dream? Of course I dream.
But not like her. No, never like her.

I do not see the tigers.
I just hear them roar. And I shiver.

Outgrown
(for Zoe)

It is both sad and a relief to fold so carefully
her outgrown clothes and line up the little worn shoes
of childhood, so prudent, scuffed and particular.
It is both happy and horrible to send them galloping
back tappity-tap along the misty chill path into the past.

It is both a freedom and a prison, to be outgrown
by her as she towers over me as thin as a sequin
in her doc martens and her pretty skirt,
because just as I work out how to be a mother
she stops being a child.

Forgive

It is easy to forgive a lot of trees
for growing all together
and just call them a forest.

A round map of the world glitters
when you forgive it,
and rivers get wetter.

It is easy to forgive children,
you can think about them, far away,
in some nice apartment in New York, say,
or Macao,

running from one big sunny room to another,
and forgive them all the time,
they are like new shoes that hurt
without meaning to…

But it is hard to forgive someone
who used to be brave
and happy and as real
as the planet we all live on

when that person
smashes up everything you own
with small cold mean hands,
and then wants kisses...

And if that person doesn't even
want to be forgiven,
is he or she worth a week
of not being able to dream straight?

Tell me what you think.
Shall the women fly, or become trees
with dark green leaves that never fall?
Is it easy to forgive trees?

When you look at trees and people
do you want to forgive them
or paint them?
Or is it all much too sad –

so that for days it doesn't matter
if you are a man or a woman,
sighted,
or blind with a golden dog for eyes?

And hoping
is like finding out what happened in the past –
not possible.

The world has so many people in it!
But it forgives them all, not hoping
for anything.

It forgives even the important ones.
They are forgiven. Just like the trees.
Call them a forest. Let rain fall on them.

Waterlily Tradition

The women are singing in the patisserie,
their faces pencilled
by doubts, diets and genre friendships,

but he composes better songs
skinnydipping beautifully in my lily pond,
lolling against the Lucida and the Perry's Pink.

I wonder what else he will do to make me
feel so strange – there are so many possibilities.

While he floats and composes like a foundling
among copulant dragonflies and sleepy slithering terrapins,
I worry that nothing will last, nothing!

But then, remembering other lives I never speak about,
I feel more cheerful, and drift out
to my trustful garden where at the waterside
young Rossini is slicking back

his damp dago curls. How honestly he consumes
my candied patronage! He takes my hand,
glad to be haunted by me, and tells me,

'Childhood is often close to the waterlily
tradition, Madame – ruthless floating innocence,
too beautiful, too observed...'

What he says must be true, I know this,
just as I know one day he will betray me.
But for today I am content to be in tune with young Rossini

who says he can smell water a mile off
like a horse, and who composes best with rain on his lips.
He kisses me...

Now do you believe me when I say I love to sing?
It is my waterlily tradition.

Worse Things Than Divorce

I was helping Dancey lift his wife April by her ears into the sky
(he was round today like someone a fish might imagine)
when a gang of blue-jeaned mothers, each with a tiny snuffling baby
floppily-strapped to her bosom, rushed us and rescued her.
That evening I surprised Dancey buttoning himself into one of her gowns.
Swathed in the soft bondage of her perilously-frail undergarments,
he said with a regal glare, 'Obviously I seek to detain her spirit,
Carol. But her perfumes are fading, minute by minute!'
He avoided red the least of all the colours in her wardrobe.
'Oh why did they take her from me!' he wept, his moustache
dribbling with tears. 'Now I am just like everyone else.' (Despairingly
he pulled one of her stockings down over his face.)

We parted friends, sometime in late summer, early autumn.
It rained and rained as he legged it past the Lloyds Building,
lovely bright rain, you know?
so that everything had this golden-wet alchemique glitter,
especially the sky rainbowing high over the city of fierce mothers
and tiny babies and disappeared wives, the sky
where Dancey longed to reign with April.
'Darling,' he shouted, scampering along. 'April, darling!'
As he splashed away, he grew taller and taller,
like somebody a spider or a baby might imagine. 'Darling!'
His yells grew fainter, his head nudged the clouds...
And me? Here I am, ironing shirts, yawning, grumbling,
grinning at the whiff of sex that sneaks into the room,
just as if Dancey were here, saying, 'Lo, it is I... Everything is OK.'

Kingdom of Tiny Shoes

We are all dead, Lucy, Cush, Kilroy and me,
but we have about five or six ghosts each.
Imagine our embarrassment, here in the next world
where everything blazes with a terrible glassy
casino glamour, where it's never dark;
because for us the great egg of time is broken.

Because we all have so many ghosts,
there's a lot of singing,
dancing, gambling, drinking, depressions,
fights, shitting and blaspheming;
one of my ghosts and one of Cush's
go in for honey-eating,
we love it, spooning, yumming, lip-licking greedily.

For a long time we all refused to accept it,
being here. Then suddenly Cush said –
Okay. Here we are. At least the drinks are free.

Even here there are winter fogs
and mists and pictures of Lenin and Jesus
on the walls. There are golf courses,
movies and divorces. More and more of us arrive.
Girls fall from the air, naked.
Old men burst up through the ground.
Proudly their shaven-head ghosts rush to meet them,
welcoming them, touring the wreckage with them.
Sometimes royal dead arrive in style, by boat.

One of my ghosts is always sad. Again K
puts his best-ghost's arms around this sad one of me
and says, 'There is no baby, you had no baby, sugar.'
'I am unwilling to believe you,' retorts this ghost,
'I am sure there is a baby,' and she goes on
looking for baby and baby's ghosts.
So far this ghost of me has found several packets
of disposable nappies and a pair of tiny knitted shoes
and this gives her hope...
The rest of my ghosts just look on, blinking and sniggering,
I'm afraid, and even Lucy taps her big fanged skull,
shrugging at such foolishness.

Three poems for my artist cousin, James Gunnell

Artist in Ink

The octopus, artist in ink,
impulsively draws eight pictures at once,
but none are portraits of dry land,
as the scuba-diving critic remarks...

There are so many ways of painting,
especially with eight arms...
Why, the octopus uses only one colour,
notes the shark, that devourer of art,
circling, never sleeping, gnawing
the leg of the diver-cum-critic...

But the octopus just inks in his seascapes,
juicily uninfluenced,
his ocean floor abstracts
endlessly octaving...

Bird-painter

The famous bird-painter hobbles by,
getting richer every step.

His pet ostrich follows him everywhere,
walking on soft white dust.

The early-summer mountains
are so beautiful and gawky

but he ignores them,
he is not a painter of mountains,

he limps round his garden
as if in the salon of Mesmer,
his pet bird watching.

The bird-painter closes his eyes,
traces his descent

through the maternal line,
for was it not

one of his long-ago mothers
who told him –

if you must paint,
first take singing lessons
from the birds.

Picasso Is Right

On my bedroom wall
Father paints a beautiful picture
of the famous river that runs beside our house.

The river is black and all the clouds,
fields, thin shimmering houses, stars,
moons and bridges are black, cool and noir.
Soon the entire wall is black.

His river-painting is so beautifully black,
so wild, so percussive,
it makes me weep, on each of my tears
is painted a tiny curled-up baby, seahorse-neat.

Father shrugs off my praise.
'Picasso is right,' says Father,
'black is the only colour.
You can fly through black!'

'But, Father, where shall we fly?'
Father smiles and looks wise.
'To one of the smaller Slavic countries,
of course,' he cries,

'where they too have chosen black
out of all the colours that are...
the colour that makes everyone weep...'

Building a City for Jamie

ONE

I am building Jamie a city with plenty palaces
but no churches, the chandeliers are very difficult.
I fix cajoling windows for Jamie,
and embroider incessant doors as best I can.
'More is needed than just love,' says Jamie.

'Build me a city,' says Jamie, 'so beautiful
I'll never want to escape from it.
Dearest one, build it for me.
Let the city rise overnight in its wonder and law.'

How Jamie's little bared teeth shine, how he hugs me!

'Build me a city it will be worth fifty winters
deciphering,' says Jamie, 'let there be fountains
to wash away the evils of man, let a great river coil
through the city for you know I pray to regain the lost favour
of water…

I want my city to happen fast!
I want to be sitting in one of my cafés now,
eating dainties on the sly…
If you are my friend,' says Jamie, 'build me a city.
Build, beloved. Build!'

TWO

I lean over the plans of the city,
explaining everything to Jamie.
Your city will have wish-bone weather,
the happiest backstreets anywhere in the world,
with houses painted in such anticipatory colours,
freshly-caught fish, lily, young-green, high-flying blue!
Here the moon will be no stranger,
a heart-shaped wall will surround Jamie's city…
Look at all this scaffolding,
the cold cages of steel, jambs and stanchions,
the webs and ichors of architecture,

dog-shat-on-sand-heaps, stacks of bricks,
sketched-out foyers, half-homes, spires sighing
and moaning to be in their rightful places...
See it all roll towards the radiance of the built, Jamie!
'Oh!' says Jamie,
opening his eyes very wide.

THREE

With my bare hands I build a city for Jamie.
It is easier than I suspected. The city flies into my hands.

Swiftly I am raising towers for appreciating the moon
in Jamie's city, and many pavilions for obtaining tranquillity.
Quickly I am building a palace for the fishes' pleasure,
where in wide deep tanks his emerald utopics
pace and dream.

Gently I am making a nine-span bridge over Jamie's river,
delicate as any living creature.
The sky that sees itself in the river's clearness
is the sky of another world, you can tell at once.

Tearfully I am building a tomb for Jamie's three favourite wives,
making sure there is a false door in the tomb wall
for the deceased ladies to come and go as they please.

And everywhere in the city I plant trees in alphabetical order.
At once they begin blossoming; almond, cherry, may and plum.

Also I make sure old things are in the city,
rusty bedsteads, cracked cups and plates, some cupboards
stuffed with old maps, balls of saved string,
stained recipe books, worn shoes, faded sheet music of rueful songs.

I say, 'There must be many sorts of things in your city,
Jamie, even the ugly and old.'
At this he bends his knees, squat-howling, 'No gods! No gods!'
and beating the air with his hands, until I bring him a cool drink.

FOUR

From one of the many tremendous roofgardens in Jamie's city
we look down at the open-air library
under its giant umbrella of blue slate. 'Any one
of those books,' says Jamie, pointing, 'might become a woman.
Between the covers, like a room of gold and crimson holidays,
sultry pages shuffle her story of white under-things.
There's the rustle of a jacket,
with quick fingers she amuses herself undoing
the black hooks and eyes of print – and not minding
her lack of brothers and sisters,
she smoothes her hands down over her naked flanks,
approving the strength of her pelvis, that narrative!
(She has arrived with no luggage, you see.)
Or will you shape her, my charmer, from my rib as I sleep?'

FIVE

In the Arbour of He Who Flees The Anger
Of His Brother, Jamie is crying.

In The Garden Of The Promise Of Rain
Jamie thinks he's burying his brother's heart.

Across The Courtyard Of The Tiny Shoes,
Jamie comes to me with quick vexed steps.
'Where is my city?' he sobs, forgetting everything.

'Where is my city
that is a copy and a shadow of heaven,
my city that smells of woman's semen,
Jamie's city?'

SIX

'This is your city, Jamie.
Here it is.'

O Jamie, you are getting sleepy and not listening!
Snuggle down in my arms,
safe in this city that I built from memory.

Tomorrow when you wake in our room of interesting squalor,
asking: 'Was there really a city, a city for Jamie?'
I'll say lightly, 'No, you were just dreaming, baby. There is no city.'

'No city!' you'll frown, shivering,
as I shake my head and lie to you for your own good,
'No city?'

No city. Of course not.

A Leaf Out of His Book

(1999)

Penelope

All is made by the design of my hand.
What I weave is where and how he travels.
He sails on glittering tides I weave.
This skein is his hero's skin.

It is I who weave the web of spears.

Legend diminished me to wife
of the house, subject to suitors
and son: but my husband's life
hung from the thread coaxing through my fingers.

I spun his yarns, wove him by day,
unwove him by night, safe from harm.
I told them it was his father's shroud.
Women still see themselves in mirrors of my name.

I bend over my loom
and throw my shuttle, weaving
the world, its weathers,
its wise and unwise ways,

weaving your names, casting my
namesakes back into the web that flows
so fast from my ravelling hands.
Over my face they pinned a veil of lies.

But it was made by the design of my hand.

Eclipse

Weather-wise, we are more anxious
than for an only child's wedding,
or an outdoor fête

at which a royal threatens to appear,
this fête of fêtes,
the eclipse, total and in preparation

for seventy years.
We need clear skies, we need
the weather to sit tight and be good.

'How can I express the darkness?
It was a sudden plunge
when one did not expect it;

being at the mercy of the sky…'
Virginia Woolf,
eclipse-watching in 1927.

As our eclipse ripens
the first landfall of darkening
will be Land's End,

one by one the b and b villages
of the Peninsula –
Madron, Zennor and Goldsithney,

Manaccan, St Keverne, Breage
and Pampaluna – will go dark. Just after
breakfast Godolphin Hill will vanish,

and then Falmouth,
so often by so many
sailed around, now to be sailed

into a rare dark
at the noon height of the beach-partying day,
by a night out of sequence,

wandering the worlds,
resistless. This is the event
that must be looked at aslant or askance,

through special goggles,
like amateur welders,
or by any curious avoidance device,

just as Dad in 1944
in his jungle prison camp at Chungkai
saw an eclipse of the sun

reflected in the water
from the River Kwai
with which speculum he'd filled his army haversack.

Scholar's Shop

He has farewells
like jewels,
he has thoughts like a tree
of thoughts,
or like little crusts of bread,
he has books of a calmness
not to be found anywhere else. Yet
he is as a false jewel
to himself, a sky unfolded without thought.
He has continuance,
like the sun or the moon.
He has Venice and Genoa
for shield and protection. He has hope
in the form of a globe. He has storms,
like riches. He assembles in crowds,
in leapyear biographies. He washes over me
in faiths of water, frosts of light,
cloud-memoirs. He shows me
how to design a peach, how to find
a landscape not yet two years old,
he is progressive as a comet,
sparkling, icy, all tail and purpose,
or wears his bird mask
to build an aviary by the sea.
He has farewells like patience,
like all the world's colours appearing before their judge.

Herbal Warfare

A wartime appeal:
send us
one thousand tons of dried nettles.

Anyone who has,
anyone who is willing to learn
herb recognition.

At once
an army of gloved gatherers
the length and breadth

of the cut-off country –
schoolchildren,
devotees, recluses,

the rank-and-file left-at-homes –
got busy harvesting
the neglect of hedges,

wastelands,
ditches which nettles love best
and where they grow best.

*

The nettle's juice
is bottle green,
melancholy's green:

from its weasel-scented seepings
comes a gift,
the dye of camouflage,

nature's counterfeit.
An 'ever-growing band
of plant enthusiasts'

sent in ninety tons
of this
'flimsy-leaved uncomfortable plant',

the Stinging, the Roman,
and the Little Annual Nettle,
eight pounds of fresh leaves

yielding less
than one pound
of the dried herb.

Remember the princess
who wove nettle shirts
for the eleven swans, her brothers?

Soon tanks snuck
in under camouflage cloaks,
soldiers wore leafgreen

invisibility uniforms,
nettle tea and nettle beer
gave their strengthening iron

to the warrior drinkers;
and in 1941
under the 'vigilant

and untiring' organisation
of Dr Butcher
the herboristes collected

over ten tons
of miscellaneous herbs –
a 'noble and most exhausting task';

but a record year
for the young British herb industry.
In 1942

one thousand tons
of Horse Chestnuts,
and as many of Rose Hips…

By now each region specialised:
Wales and the West Country
had the bounty

of foxgloves,
towering, quaintly-rosetted,
its tiny multitudinous seeds

seeking the heart:
Sussex and Rutland replenished
supplies of Belladonna,

Male Fern
hurried from Northumberland,
other shires sent Henbane,

that ugly smelly soother
of labour pains,
easer also of seasickness

for the invasion troops;
and everywhere-Yarrow, with its thousand leaves;
(backalong, Achilles

healed his soldiers with this vulnerary,
Herba militaris;)
prickly Thornapple arrived,

a narcotic, an alleviator,
like Belladonna;
efficacious Vervain

to cool fevers,
(with bunches of which
the Romans swept their altars);

and seaweed
from the coastal districts,
thirty-three tons in 1944 alone,

to help with the magical succade –
called Penicillin –
born from an alliance

of waves, storms, rocks;
saving lives and comforting many:
from two seaweeds – Gigartina and Chondrus,

garnered amid biting storms,
in salt-choked air,
slippery in stinging hands,

evasive,
a wrack of healing there –
for without this Agar Agar

herborised from the seaweed
'experimental work
would have been seriously hampered...'

So into the Ministry of Health
came the pharmacopoeia of the wild,
the amateur army

somehow overcoming
the pre-central-heating era difficulties
of finding good drying places,

dispatching the herbs upcountry
in good wellwoven burlaps,
the sacks safely tied,

or sent in tins and boxes
lined with brown paper;
comfrey's crushed leaves, mildly scented,

the paper-thin leaves of lime,
the bee-beloved lime,
nerve-soother;

a ransom of herbs
paid in time of war,
supplying 'the nation's medicine chest'.

Source of information and quotations: Florence Ransom, *British Herbs* (Pelican Books, 1949).

Verdant

Leaf masks on the portal

A mask of leaves,
secret faces,
faces under the leaves,
or of the leaves,
puzzle faces,
fountains of leaves springing,
spraying from wide mouths
whose speech is a green and silent spray,
echo of unsungness

The forest where every leaf has its own smell,
its green repertorium,
has come indoors
into the tall broad stone houses,
the barns of holiness or habit
and the faces scowl from their leaf beards,
their tendril moustaches,
the men of green, the silvanae
in from the boudoirs of thunder and forest rain,
and what they don't know about good and evil
isn't worth knowing

*

Faces of abasement?
Or
garlanded?

*

Grief
in the leaf face,
as if
saying farewell
to human form –
and feeling as they do
more human than ever,
surging back
from stone

to forest shape
and back to stone again –
to watch us
from portal,
capital,
frieze, pillar,
as if to see if we can become leaf

*

'beautiful deformities;
                    deformed beauties'
Arbor mala
            and *Arbor bona*
Tête de Feuilles
            Masque Feuillu
                        Masque Herbu

*

Human faces turning to leaves
Leaf faces becoming human
My face prickling with leaves,
acanthus, vines –
will my tongue flower?

*

leaf demons
leaf angels

leaves as if blown
into disorder
by a forsaking wind

*

Hawthorn masks
blossoming,
and tiny dragons
with tails of white may

*

Foliage faces of salutation,
hieratic, compassionate,
anticipatory –
as if about to blurt out secrets
by word of leaf mouth –

leaf-rustle-speech
A parley of green discourse

Or as if what they knew
was too much for us to bear

so they stay silent
they bear it for us
half hidden in stone
subversive among hymns
leaf-reticent
still buddhas of grief

*

Here
where nature rises up
as if to speak
yet waits and waits,
speech turned to stone

As eyes open
in the stone

and stone tongues
stretch out silence

Many faces
in the leaves

Some faces smiling
but never the eyes

Bramble sprays bursting
from ears,
from mouths…

A gout of leaves
from a mouth,
a prophecy? a promise?
leaf-logos?

*

On my way home from school
I gathered leaves, my favourites,
acacia, elm,
laid them down
at the foot of special trees,
it was comforting,
it felt right,
for I was taking a leaf
out of the green man's book

*

Face to face
with the green man,
his green mirror

*

At Winterbourne Monkton
the woman on the font
is giving birth to leaves,
she has been
mutilated
so we shall not know
she is a goddess
but
there she is,
as are the mermaids
in a church in France
whose split scaly fishtails
burst into oceanic leaf

*

Leafmasks once painted bright
as Hindu shrines

But goldleaf sometimes –
exuberant, paradisal –
still circles the faces
that are then one face

*

Our green mirrors,
reflections,
our kindred spirits,
our husbands,
our brothers,
these vernal men,
stone icons,
asleep in the stone
with eyes wide open,
green shadows, green
consorts, viriditas

*

In churches, cathedrals and abbeys
the leaf lord –

like that essential flaw in the perfect pattern
where life breaks through

*

A poet dressed in ivy
addressing his words of greeting
to the Queen at Kenilworth
in 1575; in her dress of *Amor en fleur*,
all verdant and upright
in leafy brocades of royal leisure

*

le fou conceals himself
in the fragrant field of uncut grass,
hiding and seeking

le fou,
the fool green as grass,
the no-fool he

You'll see him also
in a church by the sea,
carved in wood

dark as dusk in a forest,
eyes closed,
head hooded in a cock's comb,

fool crowned with beak,
wattle,
and pinpoint averse eye

Foolscap

Also he holds a wand
carved with his own face
again bird-hooded

When the scythe-men come
to harvest the hay,
the fool in his folly still plays

All the life flies out of the field,
mice, hares, toads, spiders,
even snails must hurry –

But le fou hides,
the curved blades seek,
cut him down to size,

fool who loves to live
but not forever
in his fool's paradise,

his blood rushing off on its fool's errand,
his cheerful bones eked out;
such is the charity of the fool,

such
is the fool's
'quality of unexpectedness...'

*

'the leaves that issue
from the Green Man's mouth
are an answering song
or incantation
in which the spirits of trees
speak to man'

*

And in London we looked up
and saw the friezes and cornices
where the leafy faces quickened
high above the fumes and despair

*

Summer Lord, May King,
yet consort of a greater

*

The green face of Osiris
after his resurrection
and his chosen life
in the underworld,
'A green thought
in a green shade'

his fingers fold fast into leaves
stalks spring from his eyes

choosing freely
to be lord of a green underworld
among the hiding and seeking souls

Background information and quotations are from: William Anderson, *Green Man*
(Harper Collins, 1990) and Kathleen Basford, *The Green Man* (D.S. Brewer Ltd, 1978).
'A poet dressed in ivy': George Gascoigne (1534-77).

Mother and Daughter

(for Z)

In those days
I was entrusted with a waterfall
purer than St Nectan

or any other
that had a woman's name,
then, as now,

between afternoon
and evening, I studied
the songs

of the young waterfall
as closely
as my own cascade-acoustics allowed,

or
as the brush-footed butterflies did,
in airy precipitant good-tempers;

for in those days
I was also an Undine,
like my waterfall child:

you could see
the wet of our footprints
race across the clouds

and how
in the throes of our rainbows
we digressed into twilight

just for the fun of it,
untroubled
by talk of the end of the world...

for a wealth of water
sheltered
this young investor of ours:

then one waterfall
went travelling far and wide,
her fountains

around her
like so many fluid suitors,
while I waited out

the puzzle of my drought
until today
when

in the rippling bowl
of her hands
she brings me lasting water.

Frogs

My frogs
maketh a noise-music for me

in the mists of an ordinary
garden. My answering dance

is a locomotion of great beauty,
sporadically applauded

by frogs. Fresh croaking begins:

Ego alas, ego alas.

Z's Gift to P

Echinocorys scutata,
sea urchin nuzzled into stone,

burrower into time,
traveller past time,

worn smooth in one of the world's
uttermost pockets or pouches,

so long under the sea,
under soft hoof of octopus,

long napping rug of giant ray,
fathomless but never out of your depths,

once regarded as a fairy loaf,
stone that if kept in the larder

promised unfailing bread,
this long-distance gift

from daughter to father
had its millionth birthday

ten million years ago,
wishes you, Dad, many happy returns.

A Future for Cornwall

Let Penzance wither on its hook.
Let the dust lick and nibble Bodmin.
Let all the windows close on Truro.
Let Falmouth stoop over.

Let cloud work out what to do with Kynance.
Let the rain select its own towns.
Let the untaught waterfalls solve
the traffic problems of Wadebridge.

Let the horses of Par forget their ambitions,
but let the dogs of Veryan
dance as they have always done.
Let the babies of Gweek forget their former lives.

Let tears be brought, at last, to Godolphin.
Let spiders overtake Redruth.
Let the sky lift her dark hands over Goldsithney.
Let St Ives be blessed with a sullen and gallant pearl.

Let the ant rule Madron,
and let the barbaric geishas of Roseland,
aloof in their blooms of saffron and bronze,
learn to like a quiet life.

Ultra Sound

But I only looked at the screen
when the doctor asked the nurse –
freeze that, will you?

And saw a smoky sea roaring
silently inside my breast,
a kneading ocean of echo-scape,

resonant-surge of sombre waves,

like the Falmouth sea
at autumn twilight, smudge
of grey surfs and bruise-black billows,

grainy shadow-sea inside me,
soundless thump
of seismic wave after wave

breaking over two black rocks,
harmless cysts,

and below, mute, storm-bleak,
the long black trembling scarp of suspect tissue.

In All Weathers

A dream cannot procure you
wealth in the world

but it has a gilt-edged tongue,
is an arguer of luminous cunning,

shares out its riches
like any friend sharing sorrows
in all weathers.

God

Green sea and blue heaven.
Hot sun and cool tree.

The complete silence of Me
reflecting on my faults.

My faults?
I sit beside them, no more, no less.

They coil and doze and bask,
half-shadow, half-snake.

While the blue heaven
and the green sea

continue to provide Me
with the ideal weather of antiquity.

Someone

(for Z)

Despite the tutelage of certain weathers,
a rainfall
terribly busy and satin polite,
the tiny art of snow,

someone thought of you, and such a thought –
like a childhood
you can use over and over again,
or that centuries-old Chinese admiration for pines.

In Hiding

Just as a dowser,
despite the hole in his fortune,

knows where the finest water lives,
and why it needs so much depth,

agua de plus belle,
so I remember you

passing for rain
in your orchard,

amid your lakes in flight,
your lapinière of light,

your usable marvels:
beginning again and again,

but hidden as water hides,
in its modest science,

until found, or unfound,
as the world on its travels

wills.

The Well at Mylor

At Mylor
the water of the well

bears the armour of the light,
it hides and escapes

and stays still
under its hood of rock

amid a galore of graves
and green leaves,

spring of fresh water
beside the sea,

a find, a treasure,
a pedigree,

no idyll
but the essential source,

now retired
from its work of sole sustenance,

living among memories
of former fame,

a saint's hand dipping in
like a taper unquenched,

coins splashing down
for reverence, not luck,

from time to time,
a self baptism,

secret and quick,
for some

prefer their ritual
out of doors,

water understands this,
and loves the brow

fanned with its body
for reasons the water easily guesses,

for it is the one who blesses,
freely,

freely it runs
its long unceremonious

caress
through my fingers,

and on my lips
tastes ferriferous,

blood-hint at the periphery,
pell-mell mint at the heart.

A Leaf Out of His Book

1

Cool climate;
a light frost followed
by the removal by thieves
of several large valuable clouds.

2

A day of rain and peacocks,
warm glooms,
some vanishings
and some tetherings.

3

Pearly manes
leaving behind
only their shadows
at dusk.

4

The first age of rain.
Taller and taller
its ladders
holding up the sky.

5

On some days
a single voyage
translates as:
tears.

6

A leaf out of his book.
So the happier it made me.
A cloud of unrewarded rain.
My young Utopian,
our child in China, so far away.
Twenty years ago to this day
her life sprang in me, new.
Her sweet mirth began.

7

Vapours, odours, woodlands.
Cool lovely times.
Original unity.
Slender downy branches
spreading upward.
Woodlands, odours, vapours.
Wet jasmine pastures,
the ashy rose.
Evening, netted and green-tailed.
And the light
holding its breath.
Bright fragments of world
still shining among the dust.
Powers exhaustible
and inexhaustible.

Spilsbury's Invention

Spilsbury's jigsaws
began as 'dissected maps',
the cheaper ones 'without the sea'.

It became a social skill.
'Just think, Mama,
she is unable to put the map of Europe together.'

First, puzzle-maps;
twenty years later, portraits of English monarchs,
for the 'instruction of youth'.

Rational amusement for all ages
in the halcyon days of the jigsaw.

Soon you could choose
between *Pilgrim's Progress*
or a more contemporary event:

Edward Oxford, in 1840, say,
firing at her Majesty
as she rode in her carriage through the Park.

Sources: the essay 'Joys of the Jigsaw' by Linda Hannas, in *The Saturday Book*, No 29.
'Just think, Mama...': Jane Austen, *Mansfield Park*.

The Rose

All the white roses in Eden
blushed red at Eve's beauty,

and in The Empress's library-garden
over two hundred roses
bushelled over trellises, arcades, arbours...

Chinese rosetrees
carried to Europe on the tea clippers,

for 'such was the international regard
for the rose'
that victorious English captains

sent on to the enemy
the roses destined for Josephine –

no olive branch,
but for the sake of the rose,
as Cleopatra drenched her sails with rose-water,

her fragrant barge travelling amusk –
and as here among the meek graves
at backwater Budoc

a late yellow rose – distant cousin
to Mrs Oakley Fisher – its roots among bone,
sends up to us

tireless edgeways puffs of perfume,
shirrs and chiffons of scent,
utterance of rose, as in Eden.

The quotation above is from *Scents and Sensibility: The Essence of Excitement*
(Max Lake, 1989).

Waterstone Whispers

Hi. Out of these swarms of books
why not let me be your own buzzing book,
your bible of the poor told in pictures,

or your humming sutras brought
so far, on foot, right,
from India to China, a twenty-year walk?

No? Then surely you'd like me
to be your Liber Studiorum,
weather-stained pages of storm and shipwreck

for happy indoor voyages,
in fact, I'll be any kind of rough guide
to anywhere you like,

but I will not be a book of condolence,
like those Dianic books in which last autumn
so many wrote what they never dreamed they'd write.

But I will be your magic book from Mexico,
grimoire of painted thoughts
where the green-plumed raingod

lives inside his house of clouds,
his thunder-tower roofed with lightnings,
kind master to his favourite bird, the roseate spoonbill.

Don't go away bookless, spend that token,
let me be your paperback zen,
your wipeclean volume of occult cuisine,

even one of these lopsided anthologies,
if I must...

And you can be my papyrus,
my Tang Dynasty scroll, my Liber Amor,
for me alone to read with more than eyes,

big boy, let's be one instantly-open book,
let's get reading.

Ours

The path smelt sensible.
It made a bow, a dusty salaam.
It did not know it was coming back to me;

secretly it thirsted,
it came back,
it was in its wooden shoes.

The path came ploughing along,
I rested myself on it,
it was smiling and suffering.

Now and then we were one.
Or followed one another about,
in places where you hold your tongue.

If we were everybody or nobody
we didn't know. We were one.

St Nectan's Fall
(North Coast, Cornwall)

Slippery gentleman, St Nectan,
breathing his own weather,

raising his own lather,
custodian of spate,

of the long precipice drop
into his black begging bowl,

white water-rope, spurting cascade,
smolt and sluice of a reverse fountain

scouring round
the basalt belly of the kieve,

gimping, looping and zinging;
a water cauldron for a saint

or a luck bath for a travelling sagesse?

On the slippery ledge,
just a juniper branch to grip,

we peer in, down,
spray roaring on our faces,

maelstrom chant,
opera whirlpool in our ears,

for Nectan's whispering water-gallery
has secrets to squander-sing,

smooch-splashing and hiss-humming down
into the ever-spilling basin

of black and shagreen rock
from which a sunlit slab of water,

beck of bright gravels, runs,
little amatory river,

no Ganges, no Orinoco,
inch-deep, quickening down

greedy and humble through the wooded gorge,
a goblet gulping its secret way.

Comock's Journey

When everything they had
fell through the sea-ice floor,
they ate their dogs.

Their best dogs they saved,
and fed them on the dog leftovers.

'The voice said, Cry.'

They ate their dogs
because sea-ice ate their rations,
their lamps, harpoons and spears,
their snow knives.

'What shall I cry?'

Out of nothing but snow and tradition
Comock and his family
rebuilt home and arctic hearth,

bred up more dogs.
It took years... nightless days,
dayless nights... At last

they travelled on (what choice?)
in a driftwood, dogbone and sealskin umiak,
sailing back

towards the Ungava Peninsula,
giving famous Flaherty one helluva
surprise...

'Forgive our rags, our shitty little boat...'
The entire family, laughing –
'private joke, Bob, between us and the ice.'

The story of the survival of Comock and his family is re-told in *Arctic Dreams*
by Barry Lopez (Picador, 1986)

Under the Weather
(for P)

Weighing a cloud in your hand,
just like a common person

or the worst traveller ever,
brushing aside the pine forest,

dreading a planetary shower,
a rainy appreciation.

Weighing a swamp, or France,
or the nick of time,

or an old woe. I love you.

Dew

'Awake and sing,
ye that dwell in dust;
for thy dew
is as the dew of herbs,
and the earth
shall cast out her dead,'
says Isaiah:
so on their way
Virgil washes
the face of the poet
with the dew that in another story
restores sight
to the blind girl Truth.

Redgrove's Wife

(2006)

Redgrove's Wife

Pity Redgrove's Wife?
I think not.

Praise Redgrove's Wife?
Why not?

Kiss n'snog Redgrove's Wife?
I dare not.

Be-jewel Redgrove's Wife?
With topaz and coral?
I will not.

Publish Redgrove's Wife?
I shall not.

(But I shall).

Forget Redgrove's Wife?
No, I have not.

Question Redgrove's Wife?
Not yet, not yet.

Confuse Redgrove's Wife?
I need not.

Fear Redgrove's Wife?
Oh fear not.

Dream of Redgrove's Wife?
Yes, night after night.

Translate Redgrove's Wife?
Why not,
she's not made of tin.

Amaze Redgrove's Wife?
Leave that to Redgrove.

Written as wedding anniversary poem for Peter two years before he died.

To Be Whispered

Like an alphabet
refusing to breed in captivity

or a holy city
left out of history,

I scatter your ashes
in the autumn tide

I'm the moon continuing to grieve for you,
your gift to the children of France,

the fire that gives the world
fifty minutes to clear its museums of every Rembrandt

If I could choose,
I'd be happy at the foot of the page

If I was twilight,
or a cliff swallow, or one of those feline spiders
you loved,

I'd follow you in your new life
as salt water,

not return to the empty house
where nothing of you lingers,

summer
shut and barred behind you,

and begin once more
to draw pictures of your absence

till it seems you're right at my fingertips
if only I can work out how to touch you

In the Kitchen

A jug of water
has its own lustrous turmoil

The ironing-board thanks god
for its two good strong legs and sturdy back

The new fridge hums like a maniac
with helpfulness

I am trying to love the world
back to normal

The chair recites its stand-alone prayer
again and again

The table leaves no stone unturned
The clock votes for the separate burial of hearts

I am trying to love the world
and all its 8000 identifiable languages

With the forgetfulness of a potter
I'm trying to get the seas back on the maps
where they belong,

secured to their rivers

The kettle alone knows the good he does,
here in the kitchen, loving the world,
steadfastly loving

See how easy it is, he whistles

Missing You

1

This year no one will ask how you voted,
or if you know the way to town

No one will call you as an eye-witness
or teach you how to train a bird of prey

No one will bring you your *New Scientist*,
try to sell you double-glazing
or tell you their secrets

People will write to you
but you won't answer their letters

The high sheriff of mistletoe
will never catch your eye again

No one will peel apples for you,
or love you more than you can bear

No one will forget you

2

I wept in Tesco,
Sainsburys
and in Boots

where they gave me
medicine for grief

But I wept in Asda,
in Woolworths
and in the library

where they gave me
books on grief

I wept in Clarks
looking in vain for shoes
that would stop me weeping

I wept on the peace march
and all through the war

I wept in Superdrug
where they gave me
a free box of tissues

I wept in the churches,
the empty empty churches,

and in the House of Commons –
they voted me out of office

3

I can't cry anyone's tears except my own,
can't teach anything but my own ignorance

I can only fall from my own mountain,
ledge by ledge

I can't rival the wasp's sting
or sew except with my needle

Like a saltwater wife,
I prise open the oyster of my loss,

hoick out the pearl of your death

4

The rainbow is not enough,
nor the flood

My eye can't see enough,
nor my ear absorb sufficient silence

January is not enough,
nor June

Books are not enough,
nor the El Grecos

Christianity is not enough,
nor Judaism

China is not enough,
nor India

Good luck is not enough,
nor absolution from the bad

Jasmine is not enough,
nor the rose

Kingdoms are not enough,
nor the oldest city in the world,

without you

5

I used to be a planet,
you discovered me

I used to be a river,
you travelled to my source

I used to be a forest,
you ran away to me

I used to be the sky,
you traipsed up mountains to touch me

I used to be a moon,
you saw by my light

I was hot coals,
you held me

I used to be an atom,
you split me

I was music,
you often sang me

6

Like a tough Polish soldier
you put your clean shirt on wet

Like a rainbow without red,
you troubled the sky

You were my sower sowing wide,
my queue dans la bouche

You loved top-knotted Islamic angels
with their steep wings of gold and blue

You preferred astronomer's weather,
sciences of the birds

You were a prayer across the Orinoco,
a Tiber fitting me to perfection

7

The sky knows everything about you
but won't tell

My questions vanish to the south-west

The sea knows something about you
but keeps silent,

my enquiries turned back on the tide

The moon knows all about you
but won't speak for a thousand years

The world, knowing all about you,
swings away on its axis,

not beating about the beautiful bush

I bide my time,
just as you warned me I would

8

I've forgotten everything
the sun and moon taught me

Perhaps they were not so wise

The world was so small
I hid it in my heart

like a woman pregnant
before she was born

I've forgotten what a painter of portraits
does with a brush,

what a musician does with tone and semi-tone,
what a gardener does with a seed,

forgotten that fire burns,
grief's disbelief never ends

9

Don't bring me the sea,
or clouds, or those packs of trees,
don't bring me night, or stars
or forthright moons, or the solitude
of the river; take away
that farmyard of cyclamen,
your flooded side-street, don't bring me
the sun, leave it where it is,
don't offer me operas or banknotes,

spider-webs peppered with dew –
I don't want a bullfight
or a cushion you've worked yourself –
I don't want anything except the past,
bring me five years ago, last winter,
the week before last, yesterday

10

I make my home in your absence,
take your smallest hope

and make it grow

I wake to the dusk of everywhere
as if assisting at my own birth

or arriving in a country
where all the rivers settle down to be ice

11

World was one word
I could not guess it

World was one gesture
I could not copy it

World was one question
I couldn't answer it

World was one song
How could I sing it?

World was one forest
I couldn't fell it

World was one bridge
How was I to cross it?

12

You're a tree's guess,
a cloud's confidence,

the continent of January,
the solitude of a comet,

a world without a wren

You're the heart of when,
the pulse of where,

sleepy as a motorway,
eager as an earthquake,

elusive as an elegy,
daring as dusk

You invent your own exit
via the black economy of poetry

13

My tamer of doves,
my alphabet of the moon,
fool of night,
harvest's welcome, the grief
of day, my blind man
and my seer,
dreamer against his will,
my furious saint,
warrior of peace

14

I won't find you in the featherbed of thought
or in the blip of the city

To find you I must be the bloodhound of love,
block capitals of the rain,

swift and slow at once,
because you'll be everywhere I'm not

Suddenly I'll be there beside you
as if all the time you'd been only four streets away

15

I'm the leopard changing my spots,
the horse led to water I must drink,

the elephant who forgets,
a silk purse sewn from the sow's ear

I'm the long long road with no turning,
the cloud without a silver lining

Mine is the last straw
that mends the camel's back,

sails us both
through the needle's effortless eye

16

Think of me
as a small backward country
appealing for aid from the far-off first world

Imagine the dirt of my shrines,
the riddle of my dry rivers,
the jinx of my cities

When you hold the full purse of autumn
or celebrate the nativity of a pear,

picture me as the hawk of spring,
a one-pupil school,
the safe-keeper of sunrise

Think of me without you,
stuck here forever between rainless May
and the drought of June

17

Your name didn't change
after your death –
many others also answered to it

After your death
the climate didn't change,
the government stayed calm

Waterfalls
remembered you forever,
remaining loyal,
looking for you everywhere,
storm after storm, teacup after teacup

18

Autumn fans its tail without you
and spring bears its burden alone

Summer, that small supernatural being,
manages without you

and winter closes your many doors

Like an interval between kings,
the year is a confusion of reds and golds,

but in the gulag of August
days are where you left them,

nights,
the same

19

Are you visiting the harems of April?
Travelling the great world of May?

Are you researching the archives of June?
Do the rains of July grieve you?

Are you saluting the landslides of August,
the independence of September?

Are you in unarmed combat with October?
Does November please you?

Is December your new best friend?
Are you hunting that grail, January?

Do you still have time for February?
Have you seen March,
celebrating the marriage of green and blue?

20

We were our own seraphs –
hours came and went
in the name of the east

All trees were the product of our love,
every bit of woodland listened to us

Ours was the tabernacle of light,
the sun our sphinx of the air

We signed the electoral register
of our hearts,

voting ourselves into office
again and again

21

I've lived with your death for a year,
that despot death, that realist,

stunned,
as if I've just given birth to a foal,
or made an enemy of the rain

All at once
you had more important things to do
than to live

Death is the feather in your cap,
the source of your fame,
my darkest lesson

This dropout year closes,
I begin my second year without you,
just me and the paper-thin world

22

The TV asks me,
how long after being widowed
before you start dating?

When China tours the world
by rowing boat,

when India is small as Ireland,

when that unbeliever water
turns to wine

23

I'm letting go of you
year by year

Today it was 1970,
tomorrow it may be 1977

There is so much of you,
you will never completely cease,

but slowly
I'm releasing some of you from me,

there's no rush, no deadline,
time doesn't matter,

its just that I can't despair forever

so I pour you away from me,
libation by libation,

as if discarding the water
from the font at Manaccan
in which an infant has just been baptised.

24

A world's daylight was not enough to keep you here,
nor the night's secret of success

Summer will never forget you,
nor friendly autumn

They'd stop at nothing
to keep you where you belong

Every afternoon reads between the lines
for news of you

and on the spur of the moment
evening welcomes you, who are never there

Next week knows his fatherland is too small for you,
and next year knows it too

No city working till late at night could keep you,
nor the happy endings of the sea

The theatre sold-out every night couldn't hold you,
nor the long disobedience of the truth

Today,
who is a shadow of his former self,
lets you go,

and so do I,
all my schools closed for summer,
silent for weeks

Poem

A poem stays awake long after midnight
talking you from room to room,

does not care that walls have ears,
las paredes oyen

A poem prefers tin to silver,
silver to gold,
gold to platinum

Every year
a poem tosses a young woman from the cliffs
to the rocky sea below

A poem accidentally sends the entire letter *f*
off to Florence

but keeps the letter *t*
in a matchbox, like a tiny contraband tortoise

Sometimes
a poem is your only daughter

busy and happy in the world,
China or Spain,
abundancia de riqueza

Like the partial Angel Gabriel
in Santa Sophia
a poem is half-gold, half-invisible

A poem will do things in England
she'll never do in France

It will take more than the ten thousand lakes
for which Minnesota is famous
to drown a poem

The poem pauses now and then
to look at nothing-much-in-particular

A poem likes scraping and burnishing
the prepared surface of the etching copper,

is frequently found note-taking copiously
from *The Fantastic Historia Animalium of the Rain*

A poem makes herself tiny as a waterbear
or a tardigrade,
a mite able to survive freezing, boiling,

able to go into suspended animation
for one hundred years, if need be

Things You Can't Post

(Royal Mail leaflet)

No prohibited drugs,
no living creatures,
(pigeons make their own arrangements),
no explosives, matches, bank-notes
(unless copies of obsolete items),
no filth.

No cathedrals, no oceans,
no thunders, no lightnings,
nothing flammable and/or obscene.
No ghosts, no trains, no dry ice,
no life-size lighthouses.
No mortbois.

You may post hope
and slowly fading emotions;
biscuits, flowers.
You may post all the opposites of filth,
almost all the varieties of the fragile,
(No fragile filth).

You may post keys, you may post locks,
maps and all that which must not bend.

By all means post concertinas,
violins, flutes.

You can't post Pathogens in Hazard Group Four,
museum corridors or false alibis,
air pockets, or the essence of Zen
or a comet or a moonbeam or a huge mirror
intended to be sent up into the sky
to reflect sunlight on the winter cities of Russia,

or filth.

You may post torn hair,
rent garments, a tape of sighs.
You can post displeasure and/or benediction,
send it by land, air or sea. You may post
a substance you know or believe to be
capable of prolonging life
indefinitely.

This item will be impounded. (Like filth).

You can't post anything infra-red
or that sharp; no ports of call
or rivers, however small.
You can't (remember) post me.
I can't post you.
But you may post as many kisses as you think necessary.

(Kisses are no longer regarded as filth).

But post nothing irretrievably precious.
Nothing that might act in real or apparent
defiance of gravity. Nothing
that might lead to the conscription
of all men between the ages of 16 and 45.

Nothing with its enormous forepaw raised in menace
and its head turned towards the observer.
Nothing that squelches.

Nothing that moans.
Nothing so shadowy it may not be grasped for delivery.

No feculence, no cloaca, no filth.

In Cornish

Owl is Ula
Star is Steren
Pyscador is a fisherman
Morrab is his coast
His rainbow is camneves
His door is darras
Mor is his sea
Lor is his moon
His ear is scovarn
His eye is lagas
His eyes are dewlagas
Blejen is his flower
His summer is haf
Hunros is his dream

There is more to his lost language
than can fit on a tourist teatowel

Task

Here's your rain,
that specialises in you

Here's your fret of looking, your silvery silvern,
your year of song, worldly with light

Here's your heart, and all that it can do
What can it do?

Here's your *ange bon temps*,
your *ange mauvais*

Here's your thought,
clouds over mountains
honouring someone

Here's your summer, slowly passing

Here's your mouth, and all that it can do
What can it do?

Here's your fear,
its restive stubborn clockwork

Here's your dream, ex libris

Here's your hand, and all that it can do
What can it do?

Here's your lovely wilding
tall and shrewd and now in bloom

Here's your Mercredi,
your Vendredi,

your house, its ups and downs,
your sky, de día, de noche,
your world and all that it can do

What can it do?

Après Un Rêve

In my Mother's Day siesta
I dreamed
a poet called me on the phone –

'I can't talk long, Penny,'
he said,
'there's a guy staying with me

who's very unhappy,
he's waited weeks for his girlfriend
to call, so he doesn't like me

using the phone,
but listen' –

Now he must be holding the phone
out to the room
as the unhappy guy plays the piano and sings –

Après Un Rêve –
far-off and faint, the most beautiful rendition
I've ever heard,

so beautiful that when he's done,
I just put down the phone in wonder
without a word

to the poet or his friend the singer.

Après Un Rêve: Song setting by Maurice Ravel.

Dukedom

He folds me in his dukedom,
draping its commemorative hills and forests
round me, casting his dukedom wide
till he's down to his very last caprice.

He folds me in his septembers worked
in ivory silk, in his seascapes of living memory.
He wraps me in his dukedom
of windfall, goldfinch and peach.
He inflicts his dukedom on me like dew on a fountain,
like a year of consents,
like a lily merchant.

He brings me a list of colours ranked in order of sleep.

With a smile taken at random
from the world's stockpile, he unfurls
his meridians, temples and folios,
folds me in his coastline, refractive and just,
doubles round me
in a popular uprising of emerald and jade,
surprises me
with his momentous green democracy,
fields, pastures.

He demonstrates by storm the properties of his echoes,
by example the heaviness of his spiders.
He wraps me in his *art du bonheur*,
in his protocols and grammars,
his guilds of water, in the gallantry
of his mistakes, and in the diagrams of his purgation.

He shawls me in a déshabillé of orchards,
in the armour of his thoughts and bones,
encircles me
with his dukedom of doors, porches and portals,
its neighbourhoods of counterpoise, ellipse and hyperbola;

he flies about me
in circumnambient marvels,
wrinkles and smoothes his maps expectantly,
swathing me in views of bridges, sheepfolds, boundaries
and elevations:

he cloaks me in leisurely lakes shining from pillar to post,
in lunar versions of his dukedom,
then pulls me into the thistledown of his physics,
his atoms pulsing.

He also makes known to me his Concept of the Round.

He lures me with his sugar factories,
tempts me with the silence of his herbarium,
its perfume-chimérique.
He wraps me in his protégé clouds,
in his skies dark as the mica sunk in granite.

He fastens his dukedom
round my throat,
the weighty balsams of its silver and gold
exciting respect, a collar of pertinence:
he plaits his dukedom into my hair,
anchorages of ruby, scruples of pearl,
adorning me with all his inferior and superior mirages.

He whispers a thousand dowries in my ear,
testing my arithmetic.
He floats his shipwreck museums up to me
from the depths.
He ravels me into his dukedom's conchology.
He brings me a list of colours ranked in order of aimance,

his dukedom
minding its own business, he says...

draping its commemorative hills and forests
around me, casting his dukedom wide
till he's down to his very last caprice,

and must turn reclusive,
lie among his riches
no louder than his own lullaby,

his dukedom no bigger than a visiting card.

Art of Vanishing

Your hand vanished first,
portrait of peasant life.

Your other hand followed suit,
unfurling, hairshirt of a snail.

Your arms simply floated away,
twin seaports named after flowers.

Who will hold me now?

In order to engrave their travels
on a cloud,
your legs left not a wrack behind.

Your torso preferred to be desert sand
blowing about in crescent-shaped storms,
an existence without intelligence,

your head and heart blazed to nothing
on the funeral pyre of an apple tree,
your eyes a mere opthalmology of ash.

You'd gone,
like that house at Porkellis
hurtling down an old mineshaft,

or a cosmonaut abandoning Mir;
brief summer leaving Gondal
or a village razed by its neighbours.

Somewhere, of course, you began again,
reappearing limb by limb,
your anti-exodus,

curious about yourself
as any pencil is
with the portrait it is made to draw.

But where? Where?

Postcards

Death quietly washing his or her hands,
counting the stones of China,
the shoes of the world to come

Many thanks for your grief,
says Death,
for your cloud and your story,
says Death

scrawling postcards
of the sunset
to all his friends

And wish oh wish you were here

An Account

Thrift is the world's riches made small
but just as real

Instead of forests, one leaf
Instead of entire coastlines, one bay

To take a dozen steps is freedom
after a long lock-down

The prison cell is also a haven,
if given value

Our travels are felt to the quick,
though we seldom go further than a mile

Thrift makes you handle every coin
not as a miser
but as a prince whose revenues are boundless

Fear

I drown water
I make ice shiver

I silence silence,
I darken darkness

I dry out the desert
and poison venom

I eclipse the eclipse,
I shock electricity

I execute death
I memorise memory

I pursue pursuit
and ask asking

I question questions
and listen to listening

I set fire on fire,
burn up the sun

I slow down time
and time speeds up

as only he knows how

The Interior

All our lovely forests
have been taken away,
and our ice-cold lakes
to which no one needed to add
a finishing touch,
our fields also, cancelled,
green and local,
and our hills drawled-over with cloud;
as for our missing river
no one has seen or heard
a thing,
only the river's passport,
thrown aside,
all we have left is the sky
leaping lightly from day to night,
we keep close watch on it,
not even its tempests give us hope,
its darkest twilights occupy us for hours

Far

Far as I was
from rain or river,

from sky or school,
from each state-of-the-art tree

Far as I was
from day or night,

from star or sea,
from voice or touch

Far as I was
from Rembrandt and Van Dyke,

from any cloud,
lake or light-strewn city

Far as I was
from Africa or Antarctica,

from sleep or solace,
from my paperless office,

from rhyme, from reason,
from word, from mouth,

from this or that,
from you

or my lost and war-torn father

The World

When you're so tired
you can't bear the world,

that's when you really begin to live,
when you're closest to the world

How difficult it is to love it,
unlike the moon at first light

carrying her weight so readily
But the world

longs for all it will never have again,
that's the world's heavyweight nature,

all its mountains have fear,
all its chasms have sadness

In rainy weary prime of life
the world endures its broad lawful wings of light,

not beautiful, not happy,
so tired you can't bear it, how the world is.

Sandgrain and Hourglass

(2010)

To a Singing Master

But who shaved, washed
and dressed you for the pyre?

Did they handle you gently,
or treat you like a piece of meat?

(Were we not one flesh?)

Who cut and sewed your shroud?
Was it clean?   Was it threadbare?

Who slammed back the doors,
raked out the ashes?

Ah my singing master,
who sings to you now?

The Keening

Yo voy a cerrar los ojos

I close my eyes –
I can see you better like this,
your head and high-domed brow,

your sea-green eye,
your eyelid, patient eyelash.

You are lost to me forever
but I am looking
at your *canst no more* temple,

your ear crammed full of silence,
singer's blank mouth,
lips, the upper, the lower,
their rue and rowan.

I feast my closed eyes
on your jaw, throat and neck,
your shoulder turned forever from the wheel,
your right arm so quietly past its prime.

Ah slowcoach,
how clearly I see
your clean-pared fingernails,
your strong wrist,

and resting heart – the vial of your heart
so long our wellkept secret...

I can't bear to look there,
even through closed eyes,
nor contemplate the rapids of your bloodstream
stemmed forever,

so I gaze at all your dear limbs...

Mine is the hard scrutiny
of the aubergiste looking down
at the small-change tip in her hand,
(though I keep no inn),
or of the captain searching no man's land
for snipers, were I a warrior.

I look at your flanks
where my smoothing hand so often lingered,
loving your human body,
and at your sex
to which we gave no nickname,
at your skin's familiar landmarks,
frecks and specks and brindles –

I yearn over the vineyard of you...
not forgetting to look
at thigh, poor knee and calf,
your feet Time is not fit to wash.

Your bones, the fallen mast of your spine,
yes, those also I see –

I'm forbidden to touch you,
for we're no longer one flesh;

I may not give you a kiss of life,
nor my westerly bring joy of rain

to your parchlands,
but I am allowed this second sight of grief.

Day and night I look –
your head, your heel, your heart –
for love blindfolded is love still.

This looking is what is called mourning,
and this is how I have learned to mourn.

The Scattering

I cast you into the waters.
Be lake, or random moon.

Be first light,
lifting up its beggar's cup.

I scatter your ashes.
Be the gale teaching autumn
to mend its ways,
or leopard so proud of his spotted coat.

Be the mentor of cherry trees.

I cast your dust far and wide,
a sower broadcasting seed:
Be wild rose or hellebore or all-heal.

Descend as a vein of silver,
never to be seen,
deep in the lynx-eyed earth.

Rise as barn owl white as dusk;
dove or raven marvelling at his flight.
Know different delights.

The Repose of Baghdad

If we ever meet again,
and I don't see how we can,
it won't be on the Avenida del Poeta Rilke
in Ronda,
or by the banks of the green Guadalquivir
or in Granada
where the sunset goes on till midnight,
it won't be in any of those houses by the sea
we called our own,
or in the Plaza Abul Beka
where the house martins feed their fledglings
in mud-nests under the sills,
or in the square
where the foal above the fountain
watches his moon shadow
on the wall of an inn old when Cervantes knew it,
and it won't be up in the mountains
where at the hottest hour of the day
one hundred thin long-faced wild sheep
pour out of a cave, as from the underworld.

If I ever see you again
it won't be in the water mirrors
of the Alhambra
or in a building
that doesn't know if it's a cathedral
or a mosque
or by the fountains of the Garden of the Poets
in the Alcazar Real
or in the dark oratory
where they keep the writing bones
of St Juan de la Cruz, gift-wrapped
in white ribbons.

And if I ever travel north,
you won't be sitting beside me
on the bus to Silverknowles,
Clovenhorn or Rosewell.

If I ever sleep with you again
it won't be in our own eager bed
or in that haunted hotel four-poster at Glastonbury,
on the drunken sleeper to Paddington
or on board the QE2 well below the waterline,

we won't sleep together
in any friend's spare bed
or on a neighbour's floor
after some burst pipe emergency
or in that hilarious sleepless bed
of our first year together,

no, if we ever meet again
(and how can we?)
it will be in a summer time has lost track of,
in a back-street *hostal*
hidden in a labyrinth of tiny white lanes,

two steps past the old Synagogue
and the dens of the silversmiths,
within the white walls
and behind the black window grilles
of *The Repose of Baghdad*,
still bearing – see it? –
its faded sign of star and crescent moon.

Taking the Drip Out

Then one afternoon
in a little private office
the consultant tells Zoe and me
there's no more to be done for you,

they're going to remove
the feeding drip, up the drug dosage,
'and he'll just slip away'.

Already high on a flying carpet
of kindly morphine dreams,
you've nothing more to say to us,
though last week you could still moan,

'get me out of here'.

In the corridor the junior doctor
asks furtively,
*'if he has a coronary arrest,
do you want him resuscitated?'*

Unanswerable question –
a few feet away, on your deathbed,
you're letting go the autumns of the future,

remembering maybe
how years ago I charmed your wart away,
pressing a lump of raw steak to your cheek,
reciting,
*'O wen, wen, o little wennikins,
Here shall you build not, here have no abode…'*
before burying the chunk of meat
in the north of our garden…

Maybe you dreamed of our modest travels.
Like Rembrandt, you never visited Rome.
Like the Master of the Small Landscape
you loved the microcosmic –

sandgrains, water droplets,
chips of granite, the exact quota of crystals
packed into a geode no bigger than an egg.

On the day they take the drip out
there's so much we don't know,
how it will be your first-born,
not me or your last-born

who'll be holding your hand
as you slip away;
we don't know how hard
the world door will slam shut after you go;

above all we don't know,
Zoe and I,
how beautiful and welcoming
the sunlit sands of Maenporth will be

(o come unto these yellow sands)

nor how the equinoctial blue sky
will watch over us,
like a witty person struck silent,
as I scatter your ashes into the bright waves,
and the sea, nature's perfectionist,
bears you away in triumph.

Edward San

Some quiet person
is translating the poems of Edward Thomas
into Japanese.

Now it rains in orchards
in the land of the haiku.

The bird of the snow
is flying over Tokyo.

A pure thrush word
spreads its calligraphic wings
over Kyoto,

an unknown bird
whistles his three lovely notes
in the woods near Kiwa-Cho.

All Japan's cherry trees
shed their petals
on the old road to Hiroshima,

where no one comes for a wedding.
The bullet train
doesn't stop at Japan's Adlestrop,

but all the birds of Japan's
North Island and South Island
go on singing.

Someone is alone
in the new house at Osaka
when the wind begins to moan,

a child with his mother
on the cliffs at Morioka
hears the bell ringing under the sea

and in the mountain gardens
of Kobe, Sapporo and Hokkaido
readers are spellbound

by two voices,
the wind and the rain.

London, Pregnant

By the end of summer,
    these last August days,
        so hot, cloudy and canine,

London is massive,
    very advanced in pregnancy,
        one enormous *ouff*-belly,

every nubile woman
    big and wise as an elephant,
        vastly expectant,

lumbering onto buses
    and trains,
        all clad in maternity lycra

stretched so tightly
    over each gigantic belly
        the navel

stands out
    like a baby thumb
        stuck out hitching through the belly wall,

hey, you can practically
    see the rest of the child
        deeply engaged within –

So big with child a city,
    so close to term
        I'm surprised

the streets aren't full
    of women squatting in labour
        or cradling

their bloodied unsullied young
    at the breast
        or biting through the sinewy

nutritious cord
        before flinging it
                to the pavement pigeons –

all London
        one mass wail of newborns
                drowning out the sirens

of police cars
        blundering at top speed
                through uncaring traffic –

every child
        named in gratitude
                for the passing tourist

pressed
        into unexpected
                spontaneous midwifery –

Jorge, Wolfgang,
        Marinka, Li Yang,
                or after the café or shop

in which birth occurred,
        Costa, Strada,
                Claire, East.

Machine

I invent a machine for grading kisses
on an approximate scale of 1 – 20

rising from (1) the air kiss on the social cheek,
to the routine kiss (4) exchanged by a pair

of experienced adulterers,
the unskilled but energetic kisses (9) of adolescents,

the nose kiss (12) given to a weary old cat,
the French kiss (14)

people are giving other people all over the world
to (20) the fieriest Don Juan kiss in all Seville

But kisses the old Soviets gave
on the Mayday parade dais in Moscow,

kisses leaving a trail of destruction
in their wake,
are unacceptable,

this machine does not have a Judas function,
take those anti-kisses away.

To the eager petit machine,
(didn't I say? you carry it in your pocket
like a Blackberry)

I bring two kisses, our first, our last –
the machine's dial tells me

they are of equal value,
grades them beyond grading;

there will always be off-the-scale kisses like this,
I realise,
if we are lucky, if we are bereft.

Sandgrain and Hourglass

Your summer wishes me well.
My sunset rushes off without a word.

You rule over a Byzantium of nettles.
I tell them rain's unfinished story.

You're dust and ashes.
My Honours List bears only your name.

I climb your castle in the air.
You listen to my stay-at-home fairytale.

You have your sandgrain
and your sorrow.

I have my hourglass
and my grief.

Look at us –
so far apart, so conjoined

no one may shed
a single tear between us.

Old Explorer

Pablo Picasso, Femme nue au collier, *Tate Modern*

You create me
        in one furious day,
                you old soul-snatcher

You fling me on the canvas,
        beating off old age
                in angry brushstrokes,

on the eve
        of your eighty-seventh birthday,
                not asking me

if I want
        this vulgar river
                spouting from my sex,

or even more rude,
        to be depicted nude,
                visible farts chuntering

from my asshole –
        Nude Woman with Necklace,
                you said,

but I never expected
        this ravaging,
                to become not so much

a living landscape
        as a slut-landscape,
                turned

into a jagged mountain range,
        my naked limbs
                a chaos of blood-red sunset

and sea-green forest –
        hey, Pablo, this is me, remember,
                your young spouse, Jacqueline,

facing the gauds of your raging palette –
  Rage, rage, against…
        You say I am

terrible and splendid
      as the Witch-Queen of Sheba,
            but why put such a sad look in my eye,

such sorrow in the crook
      of my up-bent right knee,
            why give me black rat's-tail hair,

black navel, nipples and asshole?
      But you, you bad old man of the forest,
            raging, raging against the dying of the light

just say – *it's all there*,
      I try to do a nude as it is…
            Thanks a lot, Pablo,

for seeing me as a nature goddess
      lounging flatulently
            on cushions of red and gold –

I lie on a painted divan,
      you hover over me,
            Zeus in a cloud,

Zeus in a shower of gold,
      my ancient and annihilating lover,
            I'll never take up this bed

and walk again,
      caught in the pincer grip
            of your angry love's yes and no,

you *raging against the dying of the light*
      Yet thanks to you
            I'm perfectly composed,

my perspectives
      shocked into serenity,
            any casual spectator in a gallery

looking into my jetblack eye
       will see you, Pablo,
              enraged Immortal

Behind my back,
       you conjure a vast sea
              riven with stark-white light

welling up and high-tiding it,
       then ebbing
              to richest dark blue –

You strip me bare,
       subject me to your lust for life
              till I'm just bones and blood

of landscape,
       merely *a raw sexualised*
              arrangement of orifices –
                     breasts,
                            and cumbersome limbs –

You reveal me to the core,
       leave me nothing to conceal,
              utterly *nue,*

but there are limits to your power,
       old explorer,
              despite your rage

I slip from your controlling hand
       into my own being –
              Beware – should I care to, I'll rise

from your canvas,
       crush you beneath my massive careless heel,
              like Time herself,

prisoning you
       forever
              in the world's endless gallery.

Returning a Reindeer

Here is the reindeer I stole from you months ago –
such a reindeer,
this *jieva* in her third winter, pure white,
tame, even her shadow, beautiful.

She was standing lost in thought
by the *foss*, and I just had to steal her.

I'm leaving her here outside your *kåta*...
may Mary of Lapland forgive me,
may she bless you and this lovely reindeer
and all your *raidu*,
even the barren ones, even the *heagi*
good only for hauling the sleigh.

jieva: female
foss: waterfall
kåta: home
raidu: reindeer herd
heagi: gelded reindeer

The Harper

I'm just one among millions now
in the street's city, by the sea's ocean,
by dawn's dusk and the long white nights of summer.

To stop myself thinking about all the days and nights
we'll never share,
I keep myself busy as a maternity hospital
nine months after a catastrophic city-wide power failure.

We were two among millions, oblivious of crowds,
content with our pauper-treasure,
our long-running nuptials.

But the random harper, who has but one torn tune,
has played you his tune –
now I'm just one among millions,
will never magnify the Lord again in this lifetime.

Faust

If, for you, waking is like throwing open a window in a Matisse,
no hair-shirts offered,
then know you're blessed.

If, for you, afternoons are a leisurely stroll in a Russian forest
through vistas of wild roses,
then know you're living a charmed life,
friend.

If at dusk you never see the dead boy Tsarovitch go on bright tiptoe
through the topmost branches of the bonny silver birches,
call yourself lucky.

If in the evenings you receive regular visits
from The Virgin of Tender Mercies to Evil Hearts,
do not complain about your utility bills,
the credit crunch, or the indifference of your peers.

How many of them dine, as you do,
upon nightingale breasts poached in mother's milk,
prepared for you by the pierced hands of God's Son himself?

Bread

I work hard for my nightly bread
even though I'm only a poet

I work hard at listening
to what my left hand whispers to my right,
and at folding swans back into ice

I work hard, praying for the stamina
of Chagall's favourite mistress,
or the happiness of a woman
married to a man without a foreskin

Hard I work,
scrubbing doorsteps and stairways
made of words

I eat my bread dry

I reach down, pluck my unknown grandfather
from the blackout air-raid streets
of 1941 London,
removing this Superintendent of a Work Gang
repairing the city's fractured water supply
from danger

I can do this,
although I am only a poet

White Horse, Westbury

Hang-glider over the white horse,
sun-lit rider,
gnat-small over the white tail,
flank, neck...

Green hillslope
displaying the horse,
as a green wall
holds a pure-white arras
of equine design,

a green so scarab-beetle bright
it has stopped believing
in autumn,
even though the calendar says
October's almost been and gone

I'd give a lot to be the gutsy one
who wings it like a minor dragon
over the chalk-carven horse,

to be held aloft in blue air,
skim-buffeting the thermals,
steering unwaxen wings close to the sun

who glides his rays closer day by day
to the closing stable door of winter

August 16, 1945: Yanagida surrenders and hands over command of Nakhon Pathom prisoner of war camp, Thailand, to Colonel Coates

(i.m. Jack Shuttle, 1919-2003)

It might not have gone so smoothly,
that handover,
Colonel Coates at once confining
the Japanese captors and Korean guards
to their own quarters,
ordering extra rations for the starving prisoners,
more rice, meat, vegetables,
an un-heard-of whole pomelo per man,

given that the Imperial Japanese Army
had orders to massacre
all P.O.W.s as soon as the enemy landed –
it might have been different,
no brand-new green US Army uniforms
and boots handed out (the boots cumbersome
after three and a half barefoot years,
or at best shuffling along in clompers),
no chance of tasting your first toothpaste
since captivity – *I cleaned my teeth*
a dozen times on the first day,
savouring the luscious flavour of Kolynos toothpaste,
I even found pleasure in just looking
at its distinctive yellow packet –
There might have been no flight
to Saigon
in the big Dakota,
with that hush filling the plane
as it over-flew the dead
in their jungle cemeteries below,
and where the railway ran, soon
to be reclaimed by bamboo wilderness –
If bombs hadn't fallen on Hiroshima and Nagasaki
(bombs of such magnitude
you and your comrades, who hadn't even seen
a Sten gun till that first chat
with an SAS man, were mystified
as to how such things could be),
or if such bombs had never been developed,
or if developed, never used,
and the war had dragged on through a long land battle,
you might not have sailed home
on the SS *Chitral*,
but like so many others,
on every continent,
never come home,
my mother moving deeper into her silence,
never to be my mother at all

Moonspeed

Very quickly the moon shuns
the massive domes and rounded arches
of Byzantium,
the centre-fold cities of America,
Russia's cross little citadels,
by-passes backmost lakes,
all waters, cornerstones of rivers,
moon rushing
over orchards of peach and plum,
shoving clouds before her
in a cosset of shadow,
dashing over linens
draped on tenement poles,
over all your old addresses,
skimming the brightness
from each port-of-call, carrying
tomorrow's news in her breast,
along with the latent weeping of all living things,
and glittering fast, very fast over the South Pole
where the key to understanding Art Nouveau resides,
over the great Alps
in their snowy hair-shirts
and over Europe, which she salutes in passing,
coming to rest above my garden,
bringing me, whether I like it or not,
the first rain of the summer-end.

Serious Things

Nowadays
the most serious things
come into my heart
lightly,
no dark thought
comes without its promise of light,
the way dusk
gets later all through February
until, driving maybe
towards the western shore,
you can watch the moon rise
into a sky still dazed with light.

These shadow thoughts
in my heart
are made from a sadness
that brings its own light,
spinning its round yellow moon
high into the evening sky,
so that even when night
sweeps away rocks and rock-pools,
the upper air stays vision-clear,
lifting, like my heart,
above what is lost,
up into the last of the bright
where the most serious thought
is borne up into a rich jewel of light,
a diamond on the brink
of returning to the dark matrix
from which at dawn
it will again be hewn,
polished, worn on the world's ring finger.

Moon and Sea

(for John Greening)

First she arrives by rumour,
by legend, by falsehood,
      by hope

Next she arrives by rain,
      by longing

She arrives by longing,
and as if
she can't help
      herself

She arrives by cloud,
and in a mask of
      sky

She arrives
like a craze for
      mirrors,
a fashion for
      weeping

She arrives by longing,
as if she really can't help
      herself

She comes to the sea
in a rush,
      a huff,
      a tailspin,
      a snit...

Do not call her bald, do not call her
      wild,

do not say she is not a door,
of course she is a
      door –

Do not insult her by saying
        she is anyone's
        mother –

She travels without maps,
by not giving a damn,
she comes by fullpelt
        longing

She comes at her full
with a scorpion in her hand,
a knife at her breast, a price on her
        head,

unannounced,
and not always
        welcome,

arrives with her bibles that never speak of God,
        with her bitch unicorn,
                with her heart on her
                sleeve

She arrives without witnesses,
        without fuss,
without a care in the world,
without a backward
                        glance

She came by legend, by rumour,
she came to the sea
        by inclination,
                by invitation,
                        by right,

she rested her Mary-sweet hammer of light on the sea

A Singing Man

For an instant,
you're sitting on a chair made of rivers,
at a table woven from snapdragons and sunflowers,

writing songs in invisible ink
on a page the silkworm has spun you
from hand to mouth

The world's last straw drifts by

Your study folds its wings
and carries you away

But like the dove at Bareppa
I'm wrought of iron,
can't follow you,

only offer you
my olive branch,
holding it out to the place

where you, for one heartbeat, were,
        but are no more,
my singing man who keeps his shop in his throat

'The singing man keeps his shop in his throate'
– George Herbert, *Outlandish Proverbs*, No 918

In Your Sleep

You'd talk in your sleep.
I harvested those words from the quiet of night,
from another part of the forest

In your sleep you were surrounded by women,
drifting from sagesse to sagesse,
sultan in your dream harem

Or you confronted bearded muscular rivals,
shadow-men, rival philosophers, contenders –
even asleep, you were a lover and a fighter

The phrases I garnered
were riches saved for a rainy day
I thought would never come,

but here it is –
the mizzle of dawn,
your silent ghost. Oh speak

When Happiness returns after a long absence

When Happiness returns, after a long absence,
she's a very small creature indeed,
an orderly marching ant,
scurrying beetle, or web-spinner

Let her be a spider,
learning to spin her web again,
lodging modestly behind the washer-dryer
in the back-kitchen,
earning her keep by waste disposal of flies

Let Happiness be small, busy and eight-legged
for a couple of years –
Unhappiness, step out of my house,
go back to the wilderness,
where I can't hear the rustle of your black weeds
or even the shadow of your sobs

Now, raise your game, Happiness,
slip off your spider costume,
come to me in the shape of a wren
weaving your common or garden nest

I don't ask for an outbreak of joy so major
the police are called to quell it,
just your wren-song
drawing each no-longer-endless day to a close,
chanteuse of last light,
such modest happiness I think I can bear

Unsent

(2012)

Maenporth

Here's where I saw you last,
ash, bone-shard, dust

in the sea's lap laid,
taken by the turning tide,

by spindrift and salt wave,
ocean and fathom five.

Unsent

I'm writing this letter
in a garden shut-fast to us back in the day,
hungry glances over the high wall
our only chance

of glimpsing the old poet's
courtship zone...we longed to be ushered-in,
made welcome, but previous owners
guarded their privacy...

Nowadays the place does B and B...
At last I've crossed the threshold
on a July afternoon
when grumpy cool wet summer

throws off its doldrums, shells out
sunshine unlimited, on tap...
...so I can tell you all about
this long-hidden garden,

bird-wild, bird-quiet...
There's a green ha-ha,
we didn't suspect that,
a monkey-puzzle tree the poet liked

and the pine he called 'scorpion-tail',
a fruit cage big as a row of cottages,
and a run of hens so smartly turned out and buffed
each one must have her own personal groomer,

apple trees, of course, and lime trees,
and twist paths,
one of them brings me to the look-out platform –
beyond fields and Valency valley, the sea's soft blue tread...

That's all I have to tell you
in this unsendable letter, written
while a busy-bee recording angel,
in a brighter higher garden,

writes our story,
weighing every word,
forgiving us our trespasses
and leading us from (or into) temptation...

And perhaps, to carry a theme
beyond its natural span,
you're already reading both my letter,
and, over a feathered shoulder,
the angel's edict and amen...

Hospital Song

I'm my own nurse,
my own cardiologist,
my own operating theatre,
my own MRSA

I'm the visitor
with her smile of disbelief

I'm the one in the next bed
swiftly hidden behind screens,
dying in a panic-scrum of doctors

I'm the hospital
sleepless all night,
the consent form,
the morgue

I'm the pain and the salve,
the stricken one yelling –
        get me out of here

I'm my own heartbeat
pounding on and on
        but why?
long after yours has stopped

House Arrest

No one tells me how to grieve
when the doctors
give their thumbs-down,

loosen the guy ropes
holding you to life,
withdraw your feeding tube,
stop the useless antibiotics.

No one explains about grief,
or warns me that one tear
will put me under house arrest for years.

Look. The ward nurse
bends her mild head to her paperwork.

Bloomsday

You died on Bloomsday 03,
nearly midsummer,
the day back in 57
Plath married Hughes,
under the rushed electrification
of a cloud

The wild orchids are over,
just a dry lip-reading of stems
in the old flower meadow
unploughed since 1914

Memory's travelling circus
frees its lions and tigers,
they lope into a world without bars,
and friends take me to visit
the house where you and I first met,
far from town,
in the lee of serious hills

We can't go in,
strangers live at Tregarthen Farm now,
but it's enough to be in the lane,
under February clouds,
remembering our midsummer meeting,

how my books, my ear-rings
fascinated you,
and how I, chaste
as a line of poetry it takes a lifetime to write,
let down my defences, took an endless step towards you

*

What a day to choose,
considering Joyce
was not one of your heroes
(read, yes, respected, yes,
not loved) –
why not choose Yeatsday

or Jungsday? Langlandsday
or Wallace Stevensday?
But then you didn't choose it,
it chose you, freeing you
from your month-long deathbed,
we had read you enough poems,
it seemed

Waterfall Tasting

What was it called, that drought-year waterfall in Wales?
Henrhyd? White sugarstick twirling down
against the gnarl and shine of wet black rock.
It smelt of icy melt-water even in heatwave August
when the plunge of the force
had stemmed to a piss-thin stream, disappointing
and not-rare to visiting us,
but when we caught the falling water,
poverty-wise, in the hollows of our hands,
it tasted of a strange sure-footed loneliness,
a tingle of yeast, a tickle of mint…
We drank, our disappointment vanished,
we kissed, slithered morsels of wild water
between sharing mouths,
I taste it today, your long-gone lips
on mine, tongue pushing in, rubbing,
hot, muscular, the chill of water tippling
from one mouth to another.

Cambridge

In kempt and rainy Cambridge
I retrace your steps
in the last century
through cloisters and courtyards
as if hunting out
obscure and necessary herbs
to make a love potion –
and run you to ground
in the Fitzwilliam
where among the Lucien Freuds
your shade appears
without a qualm
in portraits you never sat for...

Legacy

Leave me
a swan
and a horseshoe,

Wales
and some rain,

the ancient
and modern of love

Leave me dusk
inching over the creek,

a pair of slippers
filled with tin-tacks

to teach me
to stand on my own two feet

Leave me
the hour we lost
all those years ago,

and the plucked-out
eyes
of St Lucy

Leave me to my fate

Leave me a child
unaware of her beauty

Leave me Turner,
Monet and Whistler

Leave me the dust
Leave me the broom

The Pulse

My heart's heading straight for you,
my ruby heart.

My heart with all its departing electrons
is streaming back to you,

how fast it beats to hear itself think,
how quietly it begs permission to speak.

Heart Watch

All that year I watched my heart
like a hunter, a birder,

my heart
neither broken nor mended

In January
I saw how my heart hid
from time and tide,
from fist or caress

but in February
my heart made a fool of everyone

All that year
I lay in wait for my heart –
cold hard light of March,
ragged April evenings,
but I wasn't watching-over my heart

I couldn't believe
how stupid my heart was,

I held my tongue,
there was no window I didn't look through
for watching,
no trick I didn't stoop to

When summer came my heart flew away,
sent no word,
not from Karabalghasun
or Berlin,

but sacred-heart September
dragged my heart back, kicking and screaming

When you watch your heart all the time
you get tired and fearful,
no one helps you, no one says,
    let me take over for a while

When you're watching your heart
there's no time for anything else

Suddenly October, November, December
rush past,
if only you could close your eyes,
just for a minute

Mad Prince

He's gone
      with the wind in the willows,
            my prince

mad with love
      and song
            and science,

my prince,
      sanest of the lot,
            tilting his windmills,

gone in a handful of dust,
      with his hawk
            and his handsaw

The starlings
      whirled him away on
            ten thousand black wings

Everyone's searching
      up and down the county
            (He's not anywhere)

No cove or porth,
      no starfish or sandgrain
            has seen him or heard word...

My mad prince –
  every hill's lost and lorn for him,
    but he's flung off the world

like a staying hand,
  he wouldn't stay,
    my prince,

who knows what's become of him,
  so quiet
    in his going, going, gone…

What Are You Reading?

Summer, 1969.
You came across the room
to where I was blending-in
with the wallpaper –

  'What are you reading?'

I held the book up –
that old Macmillan 'Selected Hardy'.

I took it with me everywhere
in those days, a charm,
and, it turned out, an ice-breaker…

From that moment we never looked back,
not even on the last day
in the Renal Unit,
you propped on many pillows,
eyes open, not seeing.

Now it's too late
I look back all the time…

Decades later, here's that same book,
tattered, faithful,
a book of life carrying death, but how?

In its heart? On its back...?

It carries all it must carry
in all the ways it knows.

Lose Me

Lose me in a forest
where the moon fasts
for weeks on end

or in the desert,
where water waits for no man.

Tell me the names
of everyone you've forgotten,

write to me
on crested notepaper
from a town you've never visited.

Answer five questions
I've never asked,

touch me more tenderly
than I've ever been touched,
but only after I've been gone an hour,

say my name
in that dear voice
I never hear even in my sleep –

Do all these things,
for only the marvel of time
stands between us,

only the floodwaters
of The Dog-In-A-Doublet Sluice
divide us,

only a lintel of perilous red,
fresh and wet from Rothko's brush,
keeps us apart,

no more, no less.

Sleeping-in

Sleeping-in
after journeying,

then waking to an empty house,
Time that moves in circles

April's done and dusted,
May's green and white drama begins

Fair enough, mon ami

But then Time rings
the lark's song
from years ago in my ears,

we're listening
on Goonhilly's rough golden heath,

and I don't know which way to turn
out of this circle of song I'm life-lost in

One Rose

Not enough music for one song,
nor enough light for one last day.
Not enough sleep for half a night,
nor the words to make amends.
Not enough thorns for one rose,
and never enough cloth for a shroud,
no matter how often you fold and measure,
never enough veils for Salome to shed,
dancing and stripping at her leisure.

Awards

I won no awards for my tears,
despite their magnificence.

I began weeping at first light,
by bedtime
I swam like Alice in my pool of tears

      or a Jill-of-all-grief.

Tears were my dogma, my doctrine,
my trivial round and common task.

      Where do tears come from?
      Well may you ask.

      From the hair-line crack in the heart,
      the alas of words,
      the melting pot of the eye.

At Night

Every night
I brew up a dregs
of old things,
ash, spit, brine,
quick of iron,
tongue glued to its curse

I drag my thoughts back and forth
like work I hate
but dare not leave undone,
I work far into the night,
against my will,
in and out of time

and in the small hours
you seem
more full of life
than I can ever hold
in head or heart...
Bitter aloe, salt and spit

I listen to the cars
as they crest the hill
then go on down
into the quiet night

Your days pierce mine
from so far away,
they reach this quiet night
and lo their work is done

Mr Lukie

At last,
after fifteen months,
I ring Mr Lukie,
we arrange a time,

now he's on my doorstep,
cradling,
in the discreet crook
of his professional arm,
an object wrapped in a red velvet drawstring bag.

I'm tear-startled by the weight
when he hands over
a plastic urn
shaped like an old-fashioned jar of gob-stoppers,

tell him
I'm going to scatter your ashes
in the sea off Maenporth on Saturday.

'Strictly speaking,' he says,
'you need the county council's permission,
but everyone ignores that.'

Then he asks,
'Will you be alone, on Saturday?'

'No, there'll be our daughter,
and some friends...'

...who scattered blue passionflowers
on the sands

as your ashes mingled with the saltwater...

Just as you brought nothing
into this world
so you took nothing with you,

that old thought
kept turning
its cold-comfort blade in me.

Your Three Hats

Your three woollen hats
found such pleasure in covering
your bald head.

King Solomon could have found
no more faithful servants.

Your retinue
of navy-blue Musto hats
ensured
that while two could be lost
somewhere in the house

one would always be available
        at the drop of a...
to take its rightful place
on your crown.

Letters

Some days I can't stop writing to you,
letter after letter, hour after hour.

Only by writing ceaselessly
can I keep you within reach, it seems.

There are other days
when I send you a letter no longer than one line.

These are my happiest days.

Some Mornings

Some mornings
    I wake up happy,
as if I'm still married,
    with a thousand Fridays
in reserve,
    a bit of Bach
tongue-in-cheek on the radio
    Then I glance
over my shoulder
    at the summer of 03,
realise how many days
    depended on you

Sometimes
    early in the morning
in my empty house
    I say your name
quietly, like this –
    Peter...
as if saying your name
    might raise you
from the dead
    But of course
that can never happen,
    what was I thinking...

Stock-taking

One heart, safely broken
Five Junes, long forsaken

Wardrobe crammed
with widows' weeds,
every colour under the sun

One pair of shoulders, bowed
beneath the lash of time

Countless flesh wounds
Six empty bottles under the stairs

Five mirrors for watching
a poverty specialist
slip a penny in her pocket

Some troubles unshared,
unhalved

One silver ring, slowly
turning on the spit of my finger

Any number of bridges crossed –
why not take the ferry this time?

Seven oceans to be parsed of their salt,
thirty three doors to be locked,
by word, by deed

And now what rhymes with Beelzebub?
Aye there's the rub

Span

When your dad died
you picked your way through the sadness and guilt
by setting yourself

the task of reading The Old Testament
in its entirety,
from Genesis to Malachi,

saluting and defying the old Patriarchs
in the name of the father,
(yours) and the son (you),
and the holy ghost (whatever...)

Your reward?
To live a biblical span,
three score year and ten,
no great age by today's standard.

And me? So far
my Good Book is this day,
the willow tree's blessing
my chapter and verse...

Years

You'd mock my craze for time-travel movies,
okay, I was a pushover for them,

loved to see time overthrown on the wide screen,
stuff going on behind Time's stern back,

unfailing magic to me
who yearned to sit alongside Einstein

riding that beam of light,
shooting through the pathless void.

If I could travel back to 1970,
with magic ring/fish/toad or wand,

I'd bless you with good health,
make you an offer you can't refuse,

of dying in your sleep sometime in 2032 –

then we'd time-travel together
until at last the hour-hand broke the spell.

Wish List

Must have working knowledge of weather,
loving its causes and effects

Must be afraid of own shadow
sometimes

Glass must always be half-full,
water, wine or Tizer

Must be ambitious,
yet abhor ambition

Must never think twice,
yet rue the day

Must be possessed
of patience and sobriety,

so like
and unlike you

A tall order,
stepping into your shoes

Coals

I used to walk on redhot coals.
Ah those were the days.

Now that's not pain enough,
just as weaving the shroud
wasn't labour enough for Penelope.

I had a lifelong friend once,
she whistled to her man
as she came in their door,
missel thrush across the vale.

But autumn razed her to the ground,
winter's burning fiery furnace took her,
now no bed of coals
is hot enough for my naked foot.

Day by Day

Day by day
I remember the days,

I forget the nights,
the sea, its pack of tides

Day by day
I remember the seasons,
even maytime,

and think of the universe
as a star given away
to anyone

I'm forgetting the ways
light takes pity on the world

but day by day
I remember you, I forget you,

hempen-rope smell
and throttle of grief...

and at the same time,
of course,
I'm forgetting all that

even as I remember hours
full of minutes,

no-time hours,
hours thrice-blessed,
days, nights...

my forgetting eye,
my remembering ear,
my heart, my heart, my heart...

Or another day

will not want
what you want,

will wait
for no minutes,
far as eyes can reach

Or there'll be a change
in the quiet,
your ears pricked as a gunner's

Another day
will become a day for
asking, for

glancing back
at the Great Fire
of the past

      So long since I saw you
      in the flesh,

      since the day of the week
      said my name

Or another day
will knock me for six or

change everything,
day of days in the blind room

where I see you into my arms
but no one else can see you

for you are my hand's weight,
mere soul

A Year and a Day

This is where autumn plies his trade
for a year and a day

This is where the willow weeps

This is where the sleeper
wakes for a year and a day
and the moon will be lady of all

This is where I forget you
for ever and a rainy day

This is where I lean on my shame
like a shoulder

and this is where we strike
and fold the big tent for winter

and this is how I cross the river,
The Wandle, The Ash, or The Lea

I have no luck but mine
for a year and a day

I have no name but mine
forever and a day

A voice looks down on me
what does it see
who am I to ask such a thing

Holiday

A paperclip of cloud
fastening a little rain shower
to the mountain...

Remember that holiday
on the Lleyn? 1972 was it?
Days and days of green rain
falling on a little green mountain,
I forget its name,

I forget the name of the farm
under the mountain tucked
in the crook of the county

All I remember
is waking up
in the late afternoon,
informative voices
of the Open University
on the radio,
post-coital rain
still falling,
you and I
in the lap of the gods

Pranayama

You loved your daily bout
of pranayama exercises,

your *oum* filled the house
with its peaceable thundery bass.

Nowadays I do my practice
in a roomful of friendly strangers,

we inhale through the nostril of the sun,
exhale via the nostril of the moon.

Seven years later, in our quiet house,
I sometimes hear

the measured hum of your living breath,
sidestepping the deathbed.

Say my name. Say my name. Say my name.

Love

Don't take love too seriously.
Unwatched, it may last forever,
magic carpet for domestic flights.

Don't take it all so seriously.
What's love but Shostakovich's new piano sonata?
Impatient Gilels pores over the printer's proofs,
white notes on blue paper, so dear is the music to him.

What's love, my old pal of inward perception,
but white-knuckle days, the spear-side of the family,
a peek behind the appearance of things,
nothing you haven't known about for years and years?

May Hill

I arrived at the place,
tired to my kneecaps,
to my eyebrows,
summer woods, smooth ponds,
apple orchards, kind friends,
May Hill on the horizon.
I slept like a stone,
woke tired – the others drove off
to pursuits and pleasures,
I unpacked, showered,
mooned-about, then rang
for a taxi to take me to town.
Sunday – the one taxi out
on a run to Heathrow…
I decided to walk it,
just two miles, a sunny day,
set off along a winding lane,
took the footpath,
got lost in a cider orchard,
backtracked, came out
by the lane again, followed it
till it joined a country road
round whose sharp bends
the occasional car
came close to sheering my nipples off.
After the third scare
I turned my face to the rough hedge.
Sixteen days and seven years
to the hour
since your death,
a surprise but no surprise
to learn this fact
all along the weeping lane:

>   eagle plus liver plus Prometheus plus Zeus:
>   you do the maths.

Day in London

January 2006

Everyone dressed for grief,
greys, muted colours,
even the river I cross,
heavy-slung Hungerford Bridge,
Sir Arthur Sullivan,
bleak on his plinth
in the Embankment Gardens,
you think you've had the worst of it,
reached the out-reach of sorrow,
it isn't like that,
on the river terrace
my plans for the day vanish,
people in the bus queue
recognise
the living ghost I am,
walking by the river,
then in a gallery nearby
I'm looking at paintings
of the same river, same bridges,
but done in wild colours, city
where rainbows have gone berserk,
down in the courtyard
skaters swoop round the rink,
my grief breaks out
of the icy prison I made for it,
desert wind across grey steppes
maddening people and beasts,
or a rainy season
arriving when the year doesn't expect it,
my heart chockfull of arrows
dipped in gall,
shot by ruthless Cupid,
and I'm outside again
hurrying to meet you
who will stand me up forever,
but among the memorial trees,
statues and stones of Tavistock Square

I find Virginia,
her serious blind bronze stare,
flowers and spent votive candles
before the Gandhi statue,
a square dedicated to peace,
a dad playing football
with two dark-haired boys,
their thin addict mother looking on,
strung-out, fidgety on a bench,
and others, like me,
making a temporary home here
for an hour or less,
because they're lonely,
nowhere to go,
no one to see,
sometimes you can be too troubled
to grab a twenty quid note
off the pavement,
too much in love with what's over
to take a first step
into the beckoning city,
when you can't change your life
it can be enough
to sit in a green square
and wait
(it will happen)
for the sadness
to peak and fade
into the far of your heart,
till you hear yourself say to London,
hold me up to the light, brother,
search my eyes for a single tear,
you'll not find one in a million years.

Photo

You look warily
at the photographer,
I'm more trusting,
my gaze unguarded.

A long-ago photo
taken by a stranger –
look at the grotesque size
of my white shirt collar
and the length of my hair.

Husband and wife
in a prospect of books.

Your beard's cropped short,
you look a bit of a tough lapin,
but I know your scholar heart,
how you'd take a tiny insignificant dream
from anyone,

deduce from it
an entire personal cosmology
to change the dreamer's life forever,
and mostly for the good –

I can't make out the titles of the books
on the shelves behind us,
but I hear them asking in unison –
    how long you got?
    long 'nuf to read all us guys? –

The Interpretation of Dreams –
your Freud, Jung, Marie-Louise von Franz et al –
wise books, with answers to the hardest questions,

books I've spent a week cataloguing,
ready to ship to a book-dealer,
having no more use for them,
not caring to interpret them alone.

On the Other Hand

On the other hand
just because I live alone

doesn't mean
I have to listen to Radio Four,

run scared
with a price on my head,

or seek comfort from clairvoyants,
and being a widow

doesn't mean I can't enjoy
my own green and pleasant chaos,

I walk the coast path
as late in the day as I like,

no one cares
what time I get home,

harsh liberty,
as the path brings me down

to the water at Maenporth,
asleep in its sleep,

where I'm only
a stone's throw from you –

yes, now I'm alone
I live mostly without care,

you know?

the way a solid autumn hour
carries all care within her golden fist.

Arrow

Only a leap year
can carry this letter to you.

Only the owl's now and then
will bring news of you to me.

Only a moon
unaware of her genius

can throw light
on all we have misunderstood.

Only this arrow of tears
piercing my eye

enables me to see you clearly,
as if for the first time.

Ghost of the Green Leaf

One snowy night you ask me
'Why don't your poems come from the heart any more?'

'I want logic to be my footstool,' I snap,
'the heart is too indulgent.'

You shrug at this bollocks.

Then I see your ghost body
is patterned all over with green leaves
on twining stems, beautiful incorruptible leaves,

and remember where you dwell,
Hades to the sun.

'Why don't your poems come from the heart?'

Hearts

What is it with poets and their hearts?
They leave them in the oddest places.
Such carelessness would shock the ancient Egyptians,

who kept body and soul together with such care,
knew the value of a sturdy canopic jar,
a few bandages, a peck of nitron.

But these poets. Shelley, for one.
Body-ash interred in Rome,
his Cor Cordium tucked away
in St Peter's Churchyard, Bournemouth.

And Hardy, body safe as houses in Poets' Corner,
his dried-up heart
rattling around in a biscuit tin in Stinsford,
(if indeed it is his heart).

Poets shouldn't be trusted with hearts,
especially their own.

Our Little Books

Our little books –
A5 photocopies of our poems in progress
stapled together,
fastened between covers
made from cut-down document folders,
meticulously numbered, by you.

No married couple
can critique draft-work
in the domestic arena,
among pots and pans,
bills, laundry, dust,

we had to get outdoors,
away from the hooks and pitfalls
of the house,
find a café or a park bench,
a neutral space.

Then, no longer so married,
we could speak honestly,
poet to poet...

No secret that poems of mine
have lines recast by you,
that your poems bear the fingerprints
of my close reading.

I called them *our little books*,
to be hoicked out and pored over
till a poem untangled
and became itself.

You called them *fascicles*,
bundles of words,
poems in necessary transit
from work desk to world.

Your little books are lined up on the shelf,
they stay home now,
you've left them to their own devices,
but I take good care of them,

just as you oversaw my fascicles,
your eye for dross
not sparing a line, keeping close watch
on the crucible of the poem,
its molten heat, beating heart.

Remember That Chagall

Remember that Chagall
we planned to steal?

And our first summer?
Historians regard
it as a tumultuous and eventful time.

It was.
We did everything except take control of Libya.

Remember that November afternoon
circa 1973, scheming up
new names for household paints?

Witch Custard, Robin Hood's Robe,
Goblin Beads, Snail's Labia,
Cucumber Gossip?

And the Giant of Cerne,
who took us
under his manly wing

as wildrose rain fell
from one end of Dorset
to the other?

I remember you
washing your hands
and face in the Thames,

I remember
four hundred months
of sun and rain,

our garments so often mended
they'll take no more mending
in this world or the next...

I remember life's hammer
and sickle,
how for too long
I stuck to my grief,
a fridge magnet in vain

Telling You Things

I tell you things all the time,

how lots of your ex-students came to your funeral,
what film I saw last night,

(*Silver City* – it was crap).

I tell you about the new ferry to Trelissick,
the floods at Boscastle.

You don't answer
but never mind – this one-sided conversazione
has its own magic,

like telling secrets to the bees, for good luck.

Our daughter went out for a walk
round the headland this evening –
'and everyone I passed was German'.

Yes, it's holiday season again.
Last year I slept through it,

afraid to leave the house
all that beautiful terrible summer,

not talking to you, or anyone.
Now I tell you everything,

the way the lake looked
as autumn took charge of Italy,

I can't bear you to miss anything;
Life goes on. I keep bringing it to you
for safe-keeping.

Driving Barefoot

(for Zoe)

You're driving barefoot to St Ives,
cool and calm a driver
as your father,
though it never occurred to him
to drive barefoot.
And here we are –
under the much-painted sky,
late-august relent of summer,
harbour water bright as a gull's eye.

Along the coast path
we inspect and reject unripe blackberries,
step aside as serious walkers
juggernaut by, grim-faced
with the knowledge of booted miles still to go.

And if between us,
mother and daughter,
we're lugging a coal-black slab
from Hades' mine,
chip more fit for the biggest shoulder
in the county,
we're also making light of loss,
as would he,
not being a man to linger in any dark place
longer than necessary,

and though never a barefoot driver,
one who liked, in his day,
the touch of world on unclad skin.

Before Dawn

I used to wake early, and weep.
Now I wake just as early,
calm as a cloud
in the moony sky outside.
Even thinking about unpaid bills
doesn't make me weep,
though I used to weep and weep.

4.30 a.m. No way of getting back
to sleep so I listen in
to the silence of a world dark and at rest.
I know other women
wider-awake than me.
I hear the silence beyond their weeping,
streetlamps outside their windows
won't blank out for hours and hours yet.

I used to wake early, etc…
Now I let my old friend Sleep
go his own sweet way,
listen to whoever is wide-awake in me,
running the flats of her hands
over the rough walls of the world,
looking for what?
A way in? A way out?
You tell me.

Message

You're not here – again –
in the big empty world.

But the standing stone of time
says to me –
get a life, girlfriend.

The moon is kinder,
but hints the same message
as she lingers into the dawn,

the little river
also begs me to change my tune,
as do doors, beds, tables, windows,
books, pans, pencils, socks,
loaves of bread –

all that has its place
in the big empty world tells me –
we've heard enough about your sorrow, missy...

In the Pinewoods

(for Jacqueline Glasser)

The road winds
as if forever
up through
sky-high pines,
tallest in Italy,
vast, green,
sun-shadowed,
no other cars
and us on the wrong road,
not intending to come
so far, so high,
we park
in a forest bay,
get out into breezy silence,
light spinning through
the pine-porticoes, ionic pillars
and triumphal arches
of these tall resinous beauties,
observe more than two minutes silence,
noting their sharp-enough-
to-draw-blood needles
on a perfect day for widows

Cloud to Cloud

When I couldn't
bear another day,

I cloud-watched
for dear life –
no two skies alike

Those skies
made plain to me
where my thoughts began
and where they ended

I saw the witch Kikimora
and her white Cat
scudding from cloud to cloud

*Stop weeping
on the world's shoulder!*

     Kikimora
     spat out her good advice

Night

Quiet night,
spinning quietly round me
watching and waiting

Quiet night,
two or three thoughts
flying together
to make one winged thought,
green with a dash of purple

Quiet night,
spinning its big darkness
round me,
death flies in and out
of it, death won't listen
to anyone's advice,
when you say
my name I think –
it cannot be him, how can it be

Lean Years

One year
glued to the cobwebs
of common sense.

A second year
perched
on a chair older than Egypt,
foretelling the past.

A third lean year –
bread, wine,
legends of the ordinary,

the fourth
as a silver spoon
in any traveller's mouth,

and a fifth
becoming a Roman Road girl
(I wish).

Lean year six
sat on platform four
at Doncaster Station,
waiting waiting waiting,

and my seventh lean year
leaving me no wiser
than the mermaid of Bayeux

who, like me,
never meets that Sandman
with his satchel of sleep.

Last Chance

I give you one last chance.
You don't take it,

or make excuses
in any of your many tongues,

freshwater English,
wayside Arabic,

bossy Chinese,
a scrap of Chaucer.

Light opens her fist,
lends me twelve hours.

    Pay me back sometime not soon

She winks at me.
This means I'll never see you again.

Hand

Some days
I dip my hand in,
lift you
from the big adroit swell
in the form of a sea-bright shell.

Other days,
you're an exacting nail
hammered into my open palm.

From one day to the next,
I never know what's coming,
the sea's gift,
or bloodshock shooting
from hand to shoulder to heart.

I must have what I crave,
plunge my unguarded hand
time and again
under the salty wave;
this hand will raise new lamps for old.

Ganges

Not the holy stinking corpse river
nor that curry house in Plymouth

but the old café at Mylor Creek
named after the vessel

moored here in the 1800s
as a training ship for boys

who died of its harsh regime,
the ship's bell

all that's left,
a shining brassy silence

at the café threshold,
and the inevitable sepia photo,

furled sails and scrubbed deck –
ten minutes walk away,

the house called Quibo
where Katherine Mansfield lived

for a few months in 1915
in retreat from Laurentian melodramas

at Tregarthen in West Penwith
where you and I met

in that free-at-last 1969 summer,
that love me or leave me summer...

Nights for My Left Hand

Nights for my left hand,
nights for my right.

Born-blind hours
when the dead come in
through no doors
bearing tiny proud children
in their arms.

Long past midnight
a car drives by outside,
rolled-up carpets strapped to the roof rack.

I am not *repeat not*
the author of his woes.

Linda's Dove

You'd been dead
a year and a day,
Linda came over,
we had cherries and green tea.

She told me her dream
about a dove
with diamonds woven
in his wings.

He asked for water,
then flew away
across Russia,
one hundred versts
of pine forest...

I've never seen your soul,
for Saturn owns you.

Your Room

Two desks, bed,
three filing cabinets,
wardrobe,
five manual Olivettis,
four walls of books,
so many only God
has time to read them all,
though you ran him a close second.

Correspondent of peace
embedded here –
from your sea window
you saw
yachts as oaks
escaped from the forest,
their sails
women's billowing skirts...

You'd not recognise your room,
or our house
since I've downsized,
laid the dust,
you'd be amazed
how hard I scrub and clean,
spicking and spanning.

Who's the returning Odysseus
for whom you're doing
all this spring cleaning,
Penelope?
You, of course,
home at last,
hesitant in our hallway,
murmuring,
I must be in the wrong house...

So I say –
I can't put back the swept-away dust
or unscrub the floors,
beg you to step across a threshold
swept cleaner than you ever required,
enter a house
whose open-sesame is meant only for you...

People Go to Bed

People go to bed
in Latin, in Old English,
in ethereal silence,
in Old French,
in stubborn silence

The night shows its meaning
to some,
others see only the fancy-dress
and fleeting furniture of dreams,
flashbacks of sex

People go to bed
in leap years, in Old Norse,
in sleeping cars,
slipping themselves between their hours

Then people take up their beds
and walk,
why not you?

Seven Questions

Shall we have years,
or shall we have days?

Which are better?

Shall we have weeks,
or shall we have hours?

Where's the simple minute?
Where's the year
beyond our wildest dreams?

Where's the day
that saw us through the night?

> *The Iliad* warns us –
> Love leads to War.

Shall we have days,
or shall we have years?

Days and Nights in the City

Easy to bear what's lost
in daylight, I said

Then day drifted across the city
dangling the past in pietà arms

So day comes and goes, sad as night
So night comes, sad as day
or the busker's cat-thin jig

Lead the way,
penny-whistle of silence,
through a little stony city
forgotten for years,
city I once knew well,
last place in the world
the world will think to look for me

In these small hours
the city drives stakes
into so many hearts...
who of us can rise again?

Yet at dawn
in courtyard, street or alleyway,
here we are, risen,
neither safe nor sound

Easy to bear?
said my worrybead soul,
I don't think so...

I close my door on the city,
step into sorrow's stupid arms,

the floor under my feet
mud flat, salt marsh

Sorrow, like money, never sleeps

Sorrow crooks an arm round a waterfall,
draws it near, says –
    Look, some fresh tears
    for you to cry, sweetie

I close my door,
reckon up my debts,
no one knows the sum but me
no one dares cross my black-cat path
or sees the weary-all dark place
where I lost him, it's not where everyone
thinks it is
           lilacs and the man

No one knows what
happened there but me
               what hard things were said
               and wrong things done
               never to be made good

No one knows why no light ever
or why I'll never learn if he
or how for years
I spent uncounted hours
the countless hours
carving my everyday marble judgment lips
inside the forgive-me tomb
of Arwyn Place

The Seventh Year

The seventh year
is a narrow river rushing

from bad to worse,
how can it be so hard

to bear, surely by now
loss should be as light

as a Dior scarf, a bee's wing,
a sigh?

Instead what a weighty year,
hefty as a goodbye

made of wrought iron,
a broom fashioned out of lead –

what sort of room
does such a broom sweep,
a dungeon, an oubliette?

The seventh year
has nothing to do with forgetting,

has memories the world's
strongest man would be hard-pressed

to shift, hauling a couple of
locomotives across a goods yard

childs-play compared
to tugging these memories
in its wake...

The seventh year bangs
its fist on the cell door,

drums itself out of the army,
lies about its past, forgets its future,

starts the year from scratch,
(seven year itch?), can't

believe the evidence of its eyes,
pulls out all the stops,

rescues itself single-handed
from drowning,

asks for many other crimes
to be taken into consideration,

is an eye shedding the same tear
over and over again

as the full-leaf trees
buck their great green manes
in the strong westerly

and the field shines
in a sudden bright elegy
of sunlight

Often

Often
I can't tell if I'm happy
or unhappy,

there I am,
halfway between the two,

not needing to make a decision –
happy? sad?

but in a holding zone
where happiness

keeps a shadow up its sleeve
and sorrow

is made glad
by *the pocket of time*

you and I shared
as long as the world permitted.

From Start to Finish

I love you
from start to finish,

and on days
angry as wasps.

I love you
whenever lightning strikes,
and whenever not.

I love you
teardrop by tearaway teardrop,
more than the napping Beckham,

more than April
or October.

I love you
from finish to start,

when they perform
the velvety Verdi Requiem,
and when they don't.

I love you
when I practise herbalism,
and when I don't,

whenever busy streets
rush to help me,
or not.

I love you
in this city of rivers,
saints, haystacks,

and in this village
of eternal night.

I love you
when Radio 3's on upstairs

and when Radio 3's
on downstairs,

a well of music
rising and falling through our house.

I love you
even when ten thousand widows
dare me to forget you.

I love you,
even though

(forgive me)

I threw all your shoes away
eight years ago

Too Late

I'm too late with all these poems,
too late with my word-perfect grief,

too late with my wifely wisdom,
too late with my third wish of three,

too late with hope's nil by mouth,
too late with my adieux for you.

Index

Index of titles